SO
GREAT
SALVATION

J. F. Strombeck

SO GREAT SALVATION

Understanding God's Redemptive Plan

KREGEL
CLASSICS

So Great Salvation: Understanding God's Redemptive Plan
by J. F. Strombeck

Published by Kregel Classics, an imprint of Kregel Publications,
2450 Oak Industrial Dr. NE, Grand Rapids, MI 49505.

ISBN 978-0-8254-3780-9

Printed in the United States of America

Contents

Foreword

When I was a very young believer, someone introduced me to the books written by J.F. Strombeck, and I bless the day it happened. *Shall Never Perish* settled for me the matter of my security in Christ, and *Grace and Truth* helped me understand the true relationship between law and grace. *Disciplined by Grace* balanced these doctrines for me and delivered me from the extremes some people go to when they first discover grace and assurance. I owe a debt of gratitude to Mr. Strombeck, and I gladly acknowledge it.

John Frederick Strombeck was born in Moline, Illinois, on December 16, 1881, into a pioneer Swedish family. Converted to Christ early in life, J.F. always sought God's leading in his decisions, both personal and business.

He started his own freight auditing business, which he managed for about ten years. When he was 25, he returned to school, first at Northwestern Academy, and then Northwestern University, from which he graduated Phi Beta Kappa in 1911. After his graduation, the Strombeck-Becker Manufacturing Company was born, specializing in various wood products. That same year he married.

J.F.'s first love was ministry in the church and with various Christian organizations that he supported. He served as a director or advisor to the Belgian Gospel Mission, Dallas Theological Seminary, Moody Bible Institute, Young Life, Inter-Varsity, and many others. While a member of the Evangelical Free Church, he was often invited to minister in the Word in various conferences, and he wrote many articles for Christian publications. The burden of foreign missions lay heavy on his heart, and he was a generous supporter of missionaries and schools that trained missionaries.

You will discover as you read each of his books that J.F. Strombeck, though a layman, had a thorough grasp of Bible doctrine and was able to apply it practically. He did not write books in order to *impress*, but to *express* what God taught him, so that you might enjoy the full blessings of salvation in Christ. I suggest that you keep your Bible close at hand as you read Strombeck's books, because he uses the Word from beginning to end!

Though J.F. Strombeck died on May 9, 1959, the investments he made in many evangelical ministries continue to produce spiritual dividends, and his Christ-centered books continue to challenge and instruct serious students of the Word. I rejoice that Kregel Publications is making these helpful volumes available to a new generation of believers.

WARREN W. WIERSBE

1

The Importance of Faith

GOD is Eternal, in Him are eternal values and apart from Him there are no such values. All that is of man, all that he produces and possesses, is temporal. Most human values are not only temporal, they are ephemeral. Some last a few years and others even remain for centuries for a future society to enjoy, but as for each individual no temporal values follow him beyond the portals of the grave.

As there are no eternal values apart from God, man can come into possession of these values only as he becomes related to God. Through sin, not primarily the sins of each individual, but the original sin committed by Adam, the whole human race became separated from God. Man cannot of himself through any reformation that he might bring about or by any of his own good works return to God. There is but one way for man to come to God and that is through Him Who came down from heaven and into the world as the Saviour of men. It is through the salvation that God offers in Jesus Christ, and only so, that man may become related to Him and thereby partake of His eternal values. Jesus said, "I am come that they [who will hear Him] might have life, and that they might have *it* more abundantly" (John 10:10). This life that Jesus came to give to man is eternal and the abundance of it is eternal in its values.

There is an abundant life, widely advocated these

days, but that is restricted entirely to the material and temporal. A large part of the professing Christian church has, to an amazing extent, become concerned about the abundance of the material and temporal to the exclusion of the spiritual and eternal. Moral reform, social uplift and economic problems have taken the place of the proclamation of a salvation that God freely offers to a sin-cursed human race that is traveling at a terrific speed toward an everlasting separation from Him and all that flows from Him.

Even where the need for salvation is seen and faithfully presented, very often the temporal values derived therefrom, in the form of reformed lives and remade homes, are the most loudly acclaimed, while the spiritual and eternal values that come to the individual are in many, yes, very many, instances seldom mentioned and much less given their primary importance.

The present day emphasis upon lifting the human race out of its low state has largely become one of dealing with temporal values. God's emphasis, on the other hand, as found in the Bible, is to deal with the problem of human sin and all its consequences on the basis of eternal values. This is through salvation.

Social welfare work and all moral reform, however good for the present, do not help men and women beyond the grave, and the grave is not the end of man. He has an undying soul that goes on and on and on into eternity. The salvation that God, and He alone, has accomplished through Jesus Christ provides for that undying soul of man and brings it into an unending, infinitely glorious and blissful state.

In all periods of human history has been found a recognition that there is an existence beyond the grave in which man either enjoys the pleasure of a Higher Being or suffers His wrath. Mythology is full of this concept. The American Indians looked forward to their happy hunting grounds. The Norsemen hoped to go to Valhalla. The Chinese worship the spirits of their ancestors and Hindus believe in transmigration of the soul, thinking that after death man's soul still exists, but in the body of some animal until it is cleansed and returns to God, the source of all things. Scarcely a man or woman now living does not, deep down in the heart, at some time or other contemplate a future existence.

There is also agreement that the future eternal state is determined for each individual while in the present life. When it comes to the question as to what determines the future state of each individual there is, however, the widest possible difference. On the one hand all world religions, with no exception, offer man a state of eternal bliss or relief from suffering, as a reward for something that he does. Even much of that which is called Christianity is included in this group. Directly opposed to this God offers, for the mere acceptance thereof, a free, unearned salvation irrespective of what man's sins and failures might be. He who accepts this salvation is assured eternal joy in an unbreakable union with God.

To substitute temporal values for the eternal values of God's great salvation is to miss the greatest thing that has ever been offered to man. Because a large part of the professing church leadership is doing that very thing, those outside the church, not to mention most of those inside, never hear of the eternal things which God offers freely to man, nor how these may be acquired.

Men everywhere now realize as never before the instability of temporal and material values and long for something with stability in which to trust. The only answer to this longing is found in absolute spiritual values; in the eternal values of God.

Because it is only through salvation that man can become related to God and thereby partake of eternal values, salvation must be the most important subject for man to consider.

All that is known about salvation is learned directly, or indirectly from the Bible. There is no other source for this great theme. That which the Bible teaches must, therefore, be accepted as revealing to man the meaning of salvation and how it may be acquired. In this matter man's opinions have no value. For that reason, all that is here presented closely follows the Bible's teachings.

The purpose of this book is to gather into a small volume the salient truths concerning salvation and present them in the language of the layman.

2

So Great Salvation

IT IS well, at the very beginning, to come to a clear understanding of the term salvation as here used. Webster defines salvation as 1. the "Act of saving or delivering;—preservation from destruction or calamity. 2. *Theol*. Liberation from the bondage and results of sin; deliverance from sin and eternal death." Salvation, then, is a liberation from sin and all its consequences. It is a preservation from destruction or calamity. Because it is a preservation, salvation cannot be a mere temporary experience. It is something that endures.

But salvation may include more than liberation from the bondage and results of sin and preservation from destruction. It also includes that which God does to bring man into a perfect state, a state which He has purposed for all who have been saved from the consequences of sin.

From a careful reading of the Bible it is evident that salvation does not include the same things in every age. In all ages, salvation from the consequences of sin and deliverance from everlasting death are the same. In no age does God temporarily save man and allow him to lapse back into his former lost condition. But it is in the matter of God's objective with those who are saved that there is a vast difference in salvation in the different ages.

At a time still in the future ". . . all Israel shall

be saved: as it is written. There shall come out of
Sion the Deliverer, and shall turn away ungodliness
from Jacob" (Rom. 11:26. See also Ezek. 11: 19, 20
and 36:24-28). In that salvation every Israelite, the
whole nation, becomes saved and enters into an
earthly kingdom over which the Prince of Peace
shall rule. No heavenly position is in view in that
salvation, for Israel remains an earthly people.

Another group shall be saved out of a seven year
period following the present age and preceding the
establishment of the kingdom mentioned above. At
least half of this period shall be a time of ". . .
great tribulation, such as was not since the beginning
of the world to this time, no, nor ever shall be"
(Matt. 24:21). During that period "a great multitude
. . . of all nations, and kindreds, and people, and
tongues," shall be saved. Their destiny is to be ". . .
before the throne of God, and [they shall] serve him
day and night in his temple" (Rev. 7:9-17). In God's
purpose the saved of that time shall be a heavenly
people, but they shall be *servants in His temple.*

John the Baptist spoke of himself as the friend of
the Bridegroom (John 3:29). Because he was the last
of the Old Testament prophets, this suggests that
the position of the Old Testament saints, in their
relation to Christ, shall be as the friend of the Bridegroom.

Those who are saved out of the present age of
grace (which began after the death, resurrection and
ascension of Jesus Christ and will close just before the
tribulation period begins) are said to be predestinated

to be conformed to the image of the Son of God (Rom. 8:29). They are called the body of Christ (Col. 1:24), His Church (Eph. 5:25-32). They are to become one with God the Father even as He and the Son are one (John 17:21). This is the most exalted position to which any of God's creatures shall ever be elevated.

The term salvation, as applied to this age includes, then, all that God does for man in delivering him from the consequences of sin, conforming him to the image of His own Son and in bringing him into a perfect union with Himself and His Son. This salvation is the greatest concept that has ever been given to man. It is the greatest word that has ever been written or has ever passed over human lips. No wonder that the Bible calls it "so great salvation" (Heb. 2:3).

It is salvation in this its greatest sense, as applying to the present age, and offered to those who are now living, that is considered in the following pages.

So Great Because of What It Includes

In order to place the one that He saves in this highly exalted position, God does many things for and with him. Some of these are here enumerated. They are explained in later chapters. There is deliverance from the reign of Satan, called the power of darkness, and redemption from the curse or penalty of God's holy law. All trespasses are forgiven. He who is saved becomes reconciled to God and is brought into a state of peace with Him. He is born again of God with an eternal life. He is made part of a new creation in Christ Jesus. The Holy Spirit is given to

dwell within him forever and he is also sealed by the
same Spirit. He is given a perfect standing before God
because of the merits of Jesus Christ and is placed
under the keeping and providing care of God for all
his spiritual needs. Provision is made for deliverance
from sin in his earthly life. He becomes the object of
the intercession and advocacy of the Son of God before His Father. He becomes subject to the Father's
chastening. For him there shall be deliverance of the
body from corruption and mortality. He shall be conformed to the image of the Son of God and made one
with God the Father and God the Son. He shall be
before God in love throughout all eternity.

All of these things belong to God's salvation which
He has prepared for, and offers freely to man in this
age. In these is a greatness that cannot be fathomed
by the human mind, but all may be possessed by the
mere acceptance thereof.

So Great Because Available to All Men

While salvation is not the same for all ages, in
some form or other salvation has been accomplished
for all mankind and has been made available to every
member of the human race. The following passages
show that salvation is for all men.

"Behold the lamb of God which taketh away the
sin of the world [mankind]" (John 1:29).

"For God so loved the world [all mankind], that
he gave his only begotten Son, that whosoever believeth in him should not perish, but have everlasting
life" (John 3:16).

"For the bread of God is he which cometh down from heaven, and giveth life unto the world" (John 6:33).

"And I [Jesus], if I be lifted up from the earth [on the cross] will draw all men unto me" (John 12:32).

". . . by the righteousness of one [Jesus Christ] *the free gift came* upon all men unto justification of life" (Rom. 5:18).

"God was in Christ, [on the cross] reconciling the world unto himself, not imputing [counting] their trespasses unto them" (2 Cor. 5:19).

"Who will have all men to be saved, and to come unto the knowledge of the truth" (1 Tim. 2:4).

"Who gave himself a ransom for all" (1 Tim. 2:6).

". . . we trust in the living God, who is the Saviour of all men, specially of those that believe" (1 Tim. 4:10).

"For the grace of God that bringeth salvation hath appeared to all men" (Tit. 2:11).

"Jesus . . . was made a little lower than the angels . . . that he by the grace of God should taste death for every man" (Heb. 2:9).

"And he is the propitiation for our sins: and not for ours only, but also for *the sins* of the whole world" (1 John 2:2).

"And we have seen and do testify that the Father sent the Son *to be* the Saviour of the world" (1 John 4:14).

All these passages teach the availability of salvation to every member of the human race. They do not, however, teach that all men shall be saved. It is tragically possible to reject and even neglect so great salvation and be lost forever. (See Chapter XX.)

So Great Because of What Was Required to Accomplish It

The greatness of salvation is also seen in comparing that which God did in creating the universe with that which He had to do in saving man. When God created the heaven and the earth He spake and they came into existence. "By the word of the Lord were the heavens made; and all the host of them by the breath of his mouth" (Ps. 33:6). ". . . by the word of God the heavens were of old, and the earth standing out of the water and in the water" (2 Pet. 3:5). Seven times in the first chapter of Genesis are found these words or their equivalent: "And God said, Let there be . . ." and in each case that which He commanded was brought about.

God did not only create the heavens and the earth by the power of His word; He also upholds all things by that same power (Heb. 1:3). All that man can see of the earth and all the life which is upon it, all the forces of nature and all the stars of heaven, in their respective courses, are upheld by the power of God's word. All of this reflects His omnipotence.

But God could not—and this is said reverently—by the word of His power alone bring about the salvation of man. It is true that man is born again by incorruptible seed, by the Word of God (1 Pet. 1:23), but that is possible only because of an infinite sacrificial work of God which was prompted by His love.

Why this was necessary and the effect of this sacrificial work of God will be considered in detail in Chapter VII. Here it is mentioned to show that apart from it God could not even by His omnipotence save man. Notice that in the following Scripture passages that which is done is said to be conditioned upon the giving of the Son of God and that the emphasis is upon His death.

"For God so loved the world, that he gave his only begotten Son, that whosoever believeth in him should not perish, but have eternal life" (John 3:16 A.S.V.).* Apart from the giving of the "only begotten Son" men would perish and could not receive eternal life.

"Forasmuch then as the children are partakers of flesh and blood, he also himself likewise took part of the same; that through death he might destroy him that had [past tense] the power of death, that is, the devil; And deliver them who through fear of death were all their lifetime subject to bondage" (Heb. 2:14, 15). It was through the death of Jesus Christ that the works of the devil were destroyed and man was delivered from the fear of death.

"For Christ also hath once suffered for sins, the just for the unjust, that he might bring us to God, being put to death in the flesh, but quickened by the Spirit" (1 Pet. 3:18). If Christ had not been put to death He could not have brought man to God.

* American Standard Version, commonly called Revised Version.

"Him who knew no sin he [God] made *to be* sin on our behalf; that we might become the righteousness of God in him" (2 Cor. 5:21 A.S.V.). Only as man's sins have been charged to Christ and paid for by His death can God reckon sinful man as righteous.

"Christ hath redeemed us from the curse of the law, being made a curse for us: . . . that we might receive the promise of the Spirit through faith" (Gal. 3:13, 14). Christ being made a curse for man is the condition for receiving the Spirit through faith.

"Who gave himself for us, that he might redeem us from all iniquity, and purify unto himself a peculiar people, zealous of good works" (Tit. 2:14). Apart from the death of Christ there can be none who do good works as God sees them.

". . . by the obedience of one [Jesus Christ] shall many be made righteous" (Rom. 5:19). This obedience is expressed in the following: "Who, existing in the form of God, counted not the being on an equality with God a thing to be grasped, but emptied himself, taking the form of a servant, being made in the likeness of men; and being found in fashion as a man, he humbled himself, becoming obedient *even* unto death, yea the death of the cross" (Phil. 2:6-8 A.S.V.).

The above passages declare in unmistakable terms that salvation could not have been accomplished apart from the Son of God giving His life in death.

From His exalted position in glory the Son of God spake and the heavens and the earth came into existence. When a rebellious and lost human race was to be saved, He Who had made the universe left His position in glory. He took upon Himself the form of sinful man and gave His life out in death upon Calvary's cross to deliver man from the power of Satan and redeem him from the curse (penalty) of the broken law that God might in grace save man unto Himself.

Apart from the infinite love of God as expressed in the death of His Son there can be no salvation.

But salvation is not only by the love of God as expressed in the gift of His Son. It is also by His power. Paul in writing to the Christians in Ephesus said that God exercises a power on behalf of all who believe. This power is the same as that which He exercised in raising Christ from the dead and in setting Him on His Own right hand "far above all principality, and power, and might, and dominion, and every name that is named, not only in this world, but also in that which is to come." (See Eph. 1-19:21.) Nowhere is found a greater description of God's power than this.

That which demanded the death of the Son of God and requires the fullest exercise of God's infinite power for its accomplishment, can be nothing less than "So Great Salvation."

3

So Great Compared With Creation

THE greatness of salvation can never be fully understood by man while in the present mortal body, but some of its greatness can be seen by comparing, or rather contrasting, it with creation. Both salvation and creation are God's work and His exclusively.

"In the beginning God created the heaven and the earth" (Gen. 1:1). Thus God brought all matter and all energy into existence.

The heavens are the work of His fingers, and the moon and the stars were ordained by Him (See Ps. 8:3.) This includes not only that which man can see with the naked eye, but all that lies even beyond the range of the strongest telescope. The vastness of it all is beyond the comprehension of man.

Consider next the earth with its rocks and minerals and its past life as recorded in the fossils. There are the precious stones, the diamond, the ruby, the sapphire and the emerald, each with its own special beauty and appeal to man. Then there are the marbles, granites, sandstones, limestone and slates used by man to build his houses and places of worship, amusement and business. Out of the earth man takes the ores and even the pure metals as gold and copper nuggets. By smelting and refining processes he produces metals which form the backbone of vast industrial and constuction projects. The soil of the earth when sown and acted upon by moisture and sunlight brings forth food for both man and beast.

The fossils tell their silent though eloquent story of prehistoric ages when great monsters roamed the primeval forests. And some of the forests, even in layer upon layer, remain with their massive tree trunks preserved in stone almost as hard as the diamond. The coal beds proclaim to man that ages ago there were luxuriant tropical jungles upon this earth.

All of these rocks and minerals have their own peculiar properties and each one is always the same. They are all subject to fixed and determinable laws of chemistry and physics, many of which have long been known to man and others which are being constantly discovered. It might be asked, parenthetically, how did each of the metals and minerals acquire its own individual characteristics? What gave to each metal its coefficient of expansion, its specific gravity, its fusion point, its conductibility of heat or electricity, its tensile strength, its hardness, or softness, its toughness or brittleness, and its stiffness or pliability? These are all fixed and determinable. The evolutionist tries to explain the characteristics and habits of plant and animal life by claiming chance variations from one generation to another through thousands upon thousands of generations. The laws of physics and chemistry are as complex as those of plant and animal life and the characteristics of the inorganic as fine as those of the organic. *But there are no generations to produce variations in the realm of the inorganic.* The gold and copper nuggets, the iron, lead, copper and

silver ores, and the marbles, granites, etc. are as old
as the mountains themselves. Where then did these
fixed characteristics and laws come from? There is
but one answer: God in His creative work brought
forth each element with its fixed properties and made
it subject to fixed chemical and physical laws.

Man can delve deep into the secrets of geology and
discover much but the subject is so vast that there is
much that is still to be learned.

In the same way consider plant life. How it shows
forth God's creative power! The great redwoods of
the Pacific Coast have stood there for centuries. The
firs and pines of the north, the palms of the south
and all other trees each serves man in its own way
and is always the same for there is an unchangeable
law of life within. So also the grasses that produce
grain, the plants whose roots sustain life, and others,
the leaves of which serve as food, were all given their
properties by the Creator. Still others bear flowers
that enrich the life of man as roses and lilies. Each
plant has its own habitat; the lichen on the solid
rock, the Indian pipe in the rotted trunk of a fallen
pine, the mistletoe in the high branches of trees, the
ground hemlock in the densest shade, the sagebrush
on the desert, the grains in the rich soils and open
sun, the lotus and the flags in the shallow water and
the kelp on the ocean's bed.

Yes, plant life is another great division of God's
creation that man can study and comprehend but it,
too, is so vast that even after six thousand years of

human existence upon earth there is much left for succeeding generations to learn.

So also the animal world, from the smallest of the invertebrate insects to the largest of the mammals, as the elephant and the whale, might be considered. All were made by God, each according to its kind (Gen. 1:21) whether it be the fowl of the air, the fish of the sea or the beasts of the earth or things that creep upon the earth. To these also God gave life, but of a higher order than that given to the plants. They can all move about, in the air, in the water, or upon the face of the earth. Each one of the animals has its own characteristics and fixed instincts and habits of life, and is perfectly adjusted to its own environment. Men have written books on zoology and filled libraries therewith but there is more left to learn and new discoveries are being made yearly. This, too, is but a part, and a small one, of God's creation.

Man is God's crowning work of creation. In His own image made He him, and breathed the breath of life into him (Gen. 2:7). To man God gave the power of reproduction and gave to him the earth to subdue. He also gave man dominion over the fish of the sea, the fowl of the air and all things that move upon the earth (Gen. 1:26-30).

To man was given intelligence and power of reason so that he has been able to search out many of the mysteries of creation and is daily finding more. He has learned to take the coal from out of the earth and kindle a fire under a boiler filled with water and thereby haul his heavy trains. He pumps the crude oil out of the earth, refines it and uses it to fly his planes in the air at a rate of a mile in a few seconds. By use of a broadcasting instrument and another receiving instrument man sends his voice out over the air so that men in Washington, London, Paris and Berlin carry on a conversation as though all were in one room. He uses the X-ray and examines the bones of his fellow man. He coats a film, puts it into a camera and opens a shutter for 1/100,000 part of a second and makes a complete record of all that is in front of the lens. Man looks through a telescope at the stars and the moon. He determines the speed at which light travels. He also determines the speed at which the sun and the moon travel in their orbits. Likewise he finds the motions of the earth, and from all this data he predicts years and even centuries in advance, and that to a split second, at what time there shall be an eclipse of the sun or of the moon; whether it will be total or partial, and at what place on the earth it will be visible. These serve as a few examples of what man can do. The list might be multipled indefinitely.

Why can man do all this? Because God endowed him with intelligence and because of the fixed and unalterable laws of the universe which speak of a creative intelligence and therefore of a God back of them. He who created the heaven and the earth and fixed the laws for His creation also created man with intelligence to comprehend these laws and ability to subdue the earth (Gen. 1:28).

Space has permitted the mention of but a few of the wonders of creation. The subject is beyond exhaustion yet all this and all that might be added cannot be compared in greatness with that of salvation.

That man has so subdued the creation and so marvelously used it to his own good (and likewise to evil) is evidence that its mysteries can be fathomed in a large measure by the intellect of man. But man cannot by his own intellect fathom the mysteries of salvation. They must be revealed to man by the Spirit of God. It is written, "Eye hath not seen, nor ear heard, neither have entered into the heart of man, the things which God hath prepared for them that love Him. But God hath revealed *them* unto us [who are saved] by his Spirit: for the Spirit searcheth all things, yea the deep things of God" (I Cor. 2:9, 10).

Great as it is, that which belongs to creation is finite. It can be measured by the measures of man. Gold is bought by the pennyweight and diamonds by the carat. Coal and steel are measured by the ton. Farms are sold by the acre and city lots by the front foot. Timber is valued by the thousand board feet of lumber that can be cut from it. Milk is measured by the quart and gasoline by the gallon. Transportation charges, whether by land, sea or air, are based on miles traveled. There is a depth to the sea, a height to the mountains and a breadth to the great plains. Rain falls by the inch and the temperature rises and falls by degrees. The heat content of coal is according to British thermal units. Electricity is bought by the kilowatt hour and gas by the cubic foot. Speed is measured by feet or miles per second, minute or hour. Light travels at 186,000 miles per second. The distance to the stars is measured in light years and some of them are a thousand light years away. The distance is something like this: 5,865,696,000,000,-000 miles. Great as this distance is, and beyond the grasp of the imagination of man, it is still within the limits of the finite for it can be measured by man.

There is a span of life for all living things whether they be plants, animals or mankind. It may not be more than a few fleeting moments or it may be hours, days, weeks, months or years and even thousands of years as in the case of the great Sequoias of the Sierra Nevada Range. But for each there is a beginning and there is also a certain end. Even the earth and heaven have a beginning. "In the beginning God created the heaven and the earth." But salvation is according to the *eternal* purpose of God (Eph. 3:11). It was promised before the world began (Tit. 1:2) and ". . . was given us in Christ Jesus before the world began" (2 Tim. 1:9). So also salvation shall endure after the present creation has passed away. ". . . the heavens shall vanish away like smoke, and the earth shall wax old like a garment . . . but my salvation shall be forever" (Isa. 51:6).

The creation is finite. It can be measured by measures devised by man and it can be comprehended, though incompletely, by the finite intellect of man. But upon that which pertains to salvation man can lay no "yardstick." In speaking of salvation, God always uses terms that clearly belong to the infinite.

Salvation is said to be eternal (Heb. 5:9); so also are redemption (Heb. 9:12); the life that is given to those who are saved (John 3:16) and the glory to come (1 Pet. 5:10). God's purpose in salvation is to conform man to the very image of His own infinite Son (Rom. 8:29). Forgiveness of sins is "according to the riches of His grace" (Eph. 1:7). Believers are called "to the obtaining of the glory of our Lord Jesus Christ" (2 Thess. 2:14) even the glory of Him by Whom the universe was created (John 1:3 and Col. 1:16). Though here on earth he who is saved dwells in a mortal body subject to corruption, he is promised an incorruptible and immortal body (1 Cor. 15:51-54) that shall be fashioned like unto the glorious body of his Saviour (Phil. 3:21). Salvation cannot be described otherwise than by the use of these infinite terms, terms that apply to God Himself.

To man in his original sinless state God gave dominion over the earth and all that is thereon. To those of fallen mankind who will but receive it as a free gift, God gives an infinite salvation and places them in a position far above all else in the universe (Eph. 2:6 with 1:20-22). A salvation that is so great challenges man's most thoughtful consideration.

4
So Great in View of Sin

THE wonders of salvation and its greatness are best seen in view of the awfulness of sin.

Sin originated in heaven. Lucifer, the son of the morning, the covering cherub, who was set upon the holy mountain of God, was apparently one of the greatest of God's creatures and nearest to Him. Though a creature of God he refused to be subject to Him. He rebelled against God and said, "I will be like the most High" (Isa. 14:12-14 and Ezek. 28:14).

There is much to support the thought that as a result of Lucifer's sin the earth, which was evidently his domain, was visited by a cataclysm and that therefore the so-called days of creation were really days of restoration of the old earth. For a full discussion of this interesting subject see Pember's "Earth's Earliest Ages," Chapters II and III. On the sixth day (Gen. 1:26, 27) God created man, an entirely new kind of being, that had not previously existed. Male and female created He them and gave to them dominion over the restored earth in place of Lucifer.

Man, created in the image of God (Gen. 1:26), was perfect, but Lucifer, in the form of a serpent, came to God's new creature and caused him also to sin.

To understand the awfulness of sin it is important

The Essential Nature of Sin

to see what its essential nature is—what it is that underlies all the outward manifestations of sin.

It has already been mentioned that God created man. To create means to bring forth out of nothing. While God formed man of the dust of the ground (Gen. 2:7), all that is in man that is more than a lump of earth was brought forth out of nothing. Besides that, in the beginning God created that earth out of nothing. Therefore, all that man is and has is of God. He is indebted to God for all.

He Who out of nothing could bring forth man, can also out of nothing, if need be, bring forth all that man needs. God can therefore provide all that man might need. By creating man God assumed the responsibility for keeping His creature. By preparing a garden for him (Gen. 2:8) He showed His purpose to care for man's every need. It follows then that the only rightful attitude for man, the creature, toward God, his Creator, is one of complete dependence upon and submission to Him. But the creature did not long maintain that attitude of complete dependence upon God and therein is the beginning of the long and terrible tale of man's sin.

The story of man's first sin, by which sin entered the human race (Rom. 5:12), is told in the first seven verses of the third chapter of Genesis. The serpent, i.e. Satan (Rev. 12:9 and 20:2), said to the woman, "Yea, hath God said, ye shall not eat of every tree of the garden?" In this question is a veiled suggestion to doubt God's goodness in His provision for man.

God had commanded man not to eat of the fruit of
the tree of knowledge of good and evil (Gen. 2:17).
Satan implied that in doing so God was withholding
some good thing from man.

The purpose of the question was to break down
man's perfect confidence in and dependence upon his
Creator. And that is just what it did. Instead of
trusting God, the woman began to reason about His
command. She added five words to it; "Neither shall
ye touch it." These added words made God's command seem unreasonable. She no longer implicitly
believed God's word. She was on the ground of reason
instead of faith. She looked to herself for guidance.
That is always so when man reasons about the va-
lidity of God's Word.

Only one more prompting by the serpent was
needed. He contradicted God's statement that the
day they ate of the fruit they should surely die and
then added that by eating they should become "as
God, knowing good and evil." The desire to be as
God and not need to depend upon Him could not be
resisted. The woman took of the fruit and ate and
gave to her husband and he ate. By that simple act
the creature had rebelled against God and had de-
parted from his state of dependence upon Him. In
that one act he had expressed a desire to maintain an
existence independent of his Creator. To feel that
one can do without God, or even the absence of a
feeling of the need of God, and to live without taking
God into consideration, is sin. This holds whether
the person be one of refinement and of the highest

moral standards, or one of a debased character. The good conduct of an individual is not the determining factor. It is the attitude toward God that counts. Sin, then, is essentially a setting aside of God by His creatures and taking unto themselves His place.

To depend upon self and to refuse to depend upon God alone is to refuse to honor and glorify Him as God. As a result hereof, man has gloried in himself and in his own works. This spirit of self-glory is exemplified by Nebuchadnezzar. As he walked in his palace one day he said, "Is not this great Babylon, that I have built for the house of the kingdom by the might of my power, and for the honour of my majesty?" (Dan. 4:30). It has been the spirit of man, ever since the first sin was committed, to glory in his own achievements and fail to acknowledge that all he is and has and is able to do is of God.

To refuse to remain in full dependence upon God is also to reject His will as governing in one's life, and to replace it with one's own will. This is nothing else than to depend upon one's own wisdom instead of the infinite wisdom of God.

The very essence of sin, then, is independence of God and dependence upon self. This manifests itself in failure to glorify God and in glorification of self. Man lives according to his own will instead of being guided by the will of God.

The Outward Expression of Sin

While the first sin was an act of disobedience and of theft, for man took that which was not his, these were but the outward expressions of the new attitude of independence of God. So also all acts which are called sins are but the expression and evidence of an inward nature that is independent of God.

The apostle Paul makes it clear that all kinds of sins are due to a failure on the part of man to maintain his rightful attitude toward God. Against the sinful human race he makes the following charge; "Because that, when they knew God, they glorified *Him* not as God, neither were thankful; but became vain in their imaginations, and their foolish heart was darkened. Professing themselves to be wise, they became fools. And even as they did not like to retain God in *their* knowledge, God gave them over to a reprobate mind, to do those things which are not convenient [or fitting]; Being filled with all unrighteousness, fornication, wickedness, covetousness, maliciousness; full of envy, murder, debate, deceit, malignity; whisperers, backbiters, haters of God, despiteful, proud, boasters, inventors of evil things, disobedient to parents, without understanding, covenant breakers, without natural affection, implacable, unmerciful: Who knowing the judgment of God, that they which commit such things are worthy of death, not only do the same, but have pleasure in them that do them" (Rom. 1:21, 22, 28-32). This is the awful category of sins that are but the outward manifestations of man's failure to remain in his rightful attitude of complete dependence upon God, to glorify his Creator as God, and to remain subject to His will.

There is a definition of sin which completely confirms the above explanation of the nature of sin. It is, "Whatsoever is not of faith is sin" (Rom. 14:23). Faith means dependence upon God. (See page 113.) Therefore, all that is not in dependence upon God is sin. According to this even things that seem to be good might be sin. Many think only of immoralities as sin. That is not true. The strongest bulwark of sin is not the den of vice. It is the place of self-righteousness. In the den of vice there may be a greater sense of need of God and dependence upon Him. The self-righteous feel no such need of God. They are sufficient in themselves, they depend upon themselves and are therefore far away from God though they may be highly cultured, refined and moral.

Jesus said to the chief priests and elders of the Jews, "The publicans and the harlots go into the kingdom of God before you" (Matt. 21:31).

Man Is a Sinner By Nature

There is another aspect of the sin question that is often not clearly understood. That is, man is a sinner by nature. After Adam had sinned he was not at all the same being that he was when created. By sinning he became a sinner. Adam was the only man to become a sinner by sinning. All others are born sinners. When Adam was a hundred and thirty years old he begat a son "in his own likeness" (Gen. 5:3). As Adam was then a sinner this son who was begotten in Adam's likeness was also a sinner. Everyone, except Jesus, that has since been born has been born a sinner. King David wrote, "Behold, I was shapen in iniquity; and in sin did my mother conceive me" (Ps. 51:5). That is true of every member of the human race from Adam down to the present day.

Because of this sinful nature man cannot help sinning. That is why ". . . all have sinned and come short of the glory of God" (Rom. 3:23).

Sin Is Against God

After the above discussion of sin it should not be necessary to call attention to the fact that sin is primarily against God. King David after having grievously sinned against one of his subjects confessed his sin to God and said, "Against thee, thee only, have I sinned, and done *this* evil in thy sight" (Ps. 51:4). Today there is much emphasis upon man's social relationships, and man's attitude toward God is greatly neglected. It is therefore of great importance to remember that sin, which in its essence is independence of God, is against God. Let man first recognize this and return to the right attitude toward God and then his social relationships will become right as effect follows cause.

The Marvels of Salvation

When sin is seen to be rebellion of the creature against the Creator, the desire to be independent of God and to become like God Himself independent of any other, to take to oneself glory that is due God, and to disregard the will of God, then the awfulness thereof becomes apparent. It is to this problem of sin that salvation addresses itself. "This *is* a faithful saying, and worthy of all acceptation, that Christ Jesus came into the world to save sinners . . ." (1 Tim. 1:15). Only the infinite love of God could conceive the thought of providing salvation, and that at the infinite cost of the life of His Own Son, for such a rebel creature as is man.

But the marvel of salvation becomes even greater when it is remembered that it does not only provide a restoration of that which was lost through sin. At least those saved during the present age, as has been said, are to become conformed to the very image of the Son of God (Rom. 8:29). They are to be holy and without blame before God (Eph. 1:4) throughout all eternity. They are to be one with God the Father and God the Son even as they are one (John 17:21). They shall then be "like God." They shall become that which was offered to man by the serpent, and which, in rebellion, man tried to accomplish by himself. And their place before God shall be that occupied by Lucifer before sin entered into his heart. But they are of an infinitely higher order than was he.

Salvation that forgives man's rebellion and does for him that which he tried to do for himself is well worthy of the name "So GREAT SALVATION."

5

Delivered From the Power of Darkness

WHEN Lucifer rebelled against God and said that he would set himself above the stars of God and be like the Most High he was, in the wisdom of God (which is hard for man to understand) permitted to set up a kingdom of his own over which he became the supreme ruler. It might well be called a government in opposition to that of God.

In creating man, God added a new creature to His domain. Man was a subject of God's government. To man God gave power to rule over the restored earth and subdue it to himself. Man was subject to God alone. The earth might well have been considered as a province of God's greater domain, the universe.

But only for a short time did man remain in that state of allegiance to God. He, too, rebelled. As was seen, Satan deceived man to disobey God's command. By that one act man declared his independence of God and his dependence upon himself. It was a rebellion against the government of God. In listening to Satan man yielded himself to his influence and came under his power and rule. He shifted his allegiance from God to Satan. Man also thereby surrendered to Satan the earth over which he had dominion. From thenceforth, man has been a part of the opposition government against God.

Satan's rule over the kingdoms of this world cannot be questioned. When Jesus was tempted in the wilderness, Satan offered Him all these kingdoms and their glory if He would fall down and worship him (Matt. 4:8, 9). Jesus did not contradict the claim of Satan to possession of the kingdoms of the world. They became his when man yielded himself to him. That is why John could write ". . . the whole world lieth in the evil one" (1 John 5:19 A.S.V.).

Satan's realm is characterized first of all by falsehood. Of him Jesus said, "He was a murderer from the beginning, and abode not in the truth, because there is no truth in him. When he speaketh a lie, he speaketh of his own: for he is a liar, and the father of it" (John 8:44). It was by a lie that he won the allegiance of man.

His realm is repeatedly referred to as darkness. (John 1:5, Acts 26:18, 2 Cor. 4:6, Eph. 6:12, and others). The deeds of man, as a subject of Satan's realm, are called the works of darkness (Eph. 5:11).

Men, because subjects of Satan's realm, are called children of disobedience and children of wrath (Eph. 2:2, 3). They are this because they are the children of the first man, Adam, who in the garden of Eden listened to Satan and disobeyed God. These terms are applied to all who are in Satan's realm and under his power. They are not terms that designate a particularly wicked group of persons as men judge wickedness. Jesus said to the highly respected and honored Pharisees, "Ye are of your father the devil" (John 8:44).

Contrary to popular conception, Satan is described

as a very beautiful and accomplished being. Of him it is written "Thou sealest up the sum, full of wisdom, and perfect in beauty. Thou hast been in Eden the garden of God; every precious stone *was* thy covering . . . the workmanship of thy tabrets and of thy pipes was prepared in thee in the day that thou wast created" (Ezek. 28:12, 13). Even in his fallen condition he can transform himself into an angel of light (2 Cor. 11:14). It is therefore not inconsistent with his being that his subjects be accomplished and refined and appear perfect in the sight of men.

The condition of the human subjects of Satan's realm is variously described. Of them it is said that ". . . the god of this world hath blinded the minds . . . lest the light of the glorious gospel of Christ . . . should shine unto them" (2 Cor. 4:4). They live "according to the prince of the power of the air [Satan], the spirit that now worketh in the children of disobedience" (Eph. 2:2). They are called darkness (Eph. 5:8). These are not man's words. They are God's description of mankind in the domain of Satan and under his power.

From this it is clear that man's disobedience in the garden of Eden was more than a turning away from God and a state of dependence upon Him. It was a definite turning toward Satan and an acceptance of his sovereignty for himself and his posterity. The whole human race became involved and thereby all men became subjects of Satan's realm of darkness.

Because of this condition of man, it became necessary for God to make a provision to save man from the dominion of Satan that He might save him unto Himself. That which took place when man sinned in the Garden had to be reversed.

It is significant that the first statement in the Bible that has bearing on man's salvation is a promise of One to come Who should crush the power of Satan. This promise is found in the judgment God pronounced upon the serpent immediately after he had caused man to sin. It is in these words, "And I will put enmity between thee and the woman, and between thy seed and her seed; it shall bruise thy head, and thou shalt bruise his heel" Gen. 3:15). The head is the seat of intelligence and authority, the power to dominate and rule. When the head of Satan is bruised his power is broken and thereby comes deliverance from the power of darkness. The Seed of the woman is the One born of a virgin. All others (who have been born) are of the seed of the man. "Behold a virgin shall conceive, and bear a son, and shall call his name Immanuel (Isa. 7:14). When Jesus was born of the virgin Mary the promise of a deliverer from the power of Satan was fulfilled. He came to "give light to them that sit in darkness and in the shadow of death" (Luke 1:79). This refers to none other than mankind in the darkness of the realm of Satan.

As Jesus entered upon His public ministry, on a certain Sabbath day he went into the synagogue. He was handed the book of Isaiah the prophet from which He read: "The Spirit of the Lord is upon me, because . . . he hath sent me . . . to preach deliverance to the captives [of Satan] and recovering of

sight to the blind [them that are in darkness], to set at
liberty them that are bruised" (Luke 4:18).

Jesus, the seed of the woman, did bruise the head
of the serpent but when He did so, as was also fore-
told, the serpent bruised His heel (Gen. 3:15). This
refers to the death of Jesus on the cross for it was
through death that He brought "to nought him that
had [past tense] the power of death, that is, the devil"
(Heb. 2:14 A.S.V.). In His last public discourse before His death Jesus said: "Now is the judgment of
this world: now shall the prince of this world [Satan]
be cast out" (John 12.31). "The Son of God was manifested [as the seed of the woman] that He might
destroy the works of the devil" (1 John 3:8).

When Saul [later called Paul] was stopped on the
road to Damascus he heard a voice which said "I am
Jesus . . . I have appeared unto thee . . . to make
thee a minister and a witness . . . to turn *them* [the
Gentiles] from darkness to light and *from* the power
of Satan unto God" (Acts 26:15-18).

In salvation, then, God delivers from the power of
darkness and translates into the kingdom of His own
Son (Col. 1:13). All who are saved thereby become
"fellow citizens with the saints" (Eph. 2:19). Their
"conversation [i.e. citizenship] is in heaven" (Phil.
3:20). They are no more of the present world system,
or cosmos, ruled over by Satan. They are no more
darkness, but are the children of light (1 Thess. 5:5).

6

In Him We Have Redemption

WHEN man sinned in the Garden, he not only yielded himself unto Satan and came under his dominion, he also broke God's law as expressed in the commandment not to eat of the fruit of the tree of knowledge of good and evil. The penalty for breaking that law was death. "The day that thou eatest thereof thou shalt surely die" (Gen. 2:17). That is always the penalty for breaking God's law. "The soul that sinneth, it shall die" (Ezek. 18:20).

The death that entered by Adam's sin has passed upon all men so that all men are under the penalty of the broken law (see Rom. 5:12). They are under the curse of the law.

While some reject the Bible teaching that all men are under the curse because of Adam's sin, one need not go far to find proof thereof. Every funeral is evidence of that fact. By sin Adam became mortal (subject to physical death). When Adam begat a son "in his own image" he was born a mortal. Mortal man cannot beget immortal offspring. So all men are mortal and therefore under the curse, because Adam sinned.

But that is not all. When Adam sinned he died spiritually. His spirit became separated from God. He lost spiritual contact with God. He who is spiritually dead cannot beget children that are spiritually alive. Therefore all who have descended from Adam are "dead in trespasses and sins" (Eph. 2:1). That, too, is a part of the curse of the law that has come upon man because Adam sinned. It is not true that there is a "divine spark" in every man. All, as quoted, are *dead* in trespasses and sins.

Furthermore, because of their sinful nature inherited from Adam, all men "have sinned and come short of the glory of God" (Rom. 3:23). Because of this the whole human race is guilty before God and under the condemnation of His broken law (Rom. 3:19).

In salvation then, in addition to delivering from the power and dominion of Satan, God had to make a provision for setting man free from death, that is, from the curse of the law. As death came by sin, death being the penalty because of sin, it was also necessary that man be liberated or set free from sin. Both the penalty and the cause of it must be dealt with. This provision of God is called redemption.

According to Webster, to redeem means "to ransom, liberate, or rescue from captivity or bondage, or from any obligation or liability to suffer or to be forfeited, by paying a price or a ransom." There are two parts to redemption. First, to ransom or liberate from captivity or bondage, and second, to ransom from liability to suffer and to forfeit by the payment of a price. Both of these aspects of redemption are found in God's work of salvation.

Man is in bondage of sin and is under liability to suffer the death penalty demanded by the broken law. He must forfeit his life to satisfy the demands of justice. The only way to escape judgment is by redemption.

As the penalty for the offense is death, it is impossible for man to redeem himself. His own life is greater than anything that he might offer as a redemption price. If the sentence had been an imprisonment for a term of years it might have been set aside by the payment of a given amount of good works or penance, but all the good works of a life cannot be a redemption price when the liability or obligation calls for payment by death, or the surrender of life itself. Surely there is nothing in man whereby he can redeem himself from under the curse of the law. Because all men are under the same condemnation no human help is available.

What is more, it is impossible for God, the Judge, to exercise leniency and set aside the judgment. He is infinite in all that He is and does. His righteousness is therefore also infinite. He cannot compromise in His judgments and in their execution. He cannot set aside the penalty of His Own holy law. It must be exacted.

Because man has not that wherewith to redeem himself and because God's infinite justice prevents the penalty from being set aside, if man is to be saved there must be found a redeemer. There must be found one who is able to pay a price, or ransom, that is equal to the penalty demanded by the law. Redemption then, is a very vital part of salvation. *There can be no salvation apart from redemption.*

Necessarily, under these conditions God alone can find a redeemer. This He did in the person of His Own infinite Son. For that purpose He sent His

Only begotten Son into the world to become a man. "But when the fulness of the time was come, God sent forth his Son, made of a woman, made under the law, to redeem them that were under the law" (Gal. 4:4, 5).

By His coming into the world and dying "Christ hath redeemed us from the curse of the law, being made a curse for us" (Gal. 3:13). Yes, the infinite Son of God was appointed by God to become the Redeemer of the world.

The redemption price that He paid as a ransom for mankind had to be greater, not than the life of one man, but greater than the lives of all the members of the human race for all were under the condemnation of death. And so it was, for the ransom price that He paid was His own life. He said of Himself, ". . . the Son of man came . . . to give his life a ransom for many" (Matt. 20:28). He ". . . gave himself a ransom for all" (1 Tim. 2:6).

The sufficiency of this ransom price is due to three conditions. (1) It was a human life. The broken law demanded that *man* should die. That is why the Son of God had to take upon Himself humanity. (2) His life was sinless. He could say to the Jews, "Which of you convinceth me of sin?" (John 8:46). He did not have to die because of any sin He had committed. He could therefore die for others. (3) Being the Son of God He was infinite. His life was greater than the sum total of all finite human lives. That is why His life could be a ransom for *all*—all mankind. The ransom price *was* greater than the sum total of all human sin.

It is important to notice that Jesus said that He had come to *give* His life as a ransom. He did not, as is so often claimed, die as a martyr for a cause. He *gave* His life. He said, "I lay down my life, that I might take it again. No man taketh it from me, but I lay it down of myself" (John 10:17, 18). The death of Jesus was a voluntary giving of His life as a ransom price, to redeem the human race from under the death penalty of the law.

In several Bible passages the blood of Christ is said to be the redemption price. So in 1 Peter 1:18, 19, A.S.V. ". . . ye were redeemed, not with corruptible things, with silver or gold, from your vain manner of life handed down from your fathers; but with precious blood, as of a lamb without blemish and without spot, *even the blood* of Christ." The fact that redemption is by the blood of Jesus Christ is also taught in Ephesians 1:7, Colossians 1:14, 20 and Revelation 5:9.

There is no contradiction between the two statements that redemption is by the blood of Jesus Christ and that He gave His life as the ransom price. They mean the same thing because the life is in the blood (Lev. 17:11) and when the blood is shed the life is given. That is why the emphasis must be placed upon the *shed* blood as Jesus Himself did. When instituting the Lord's Supper He took the cup of wine and said, ". . . this is my blood . . . which is shed for many

for the remission of sins" (Matt. 26:28). It is therefore
most definitely not by His life as He lived it that men
are redeemed from the curse of the law. It is by the
giving up of the life, by the shedding of blood and
therefore by His death that man is redeemed.

The meaning of all this is that man is guilty by the
law and under the sentence of death. Man has not
that wherewith he can redeem himself and escape
execution of the sentence. The Son of God came to
earth and became a man. He lived a perfectly righteous life in the sight of God's law and could have returned to heaven and come into the presence of God
because of His own righteousness. Instead of so doing
He, the sinless one, died on behalf of the human race.
He paid the death penalty on behalf of man.

Some teach that the blood of Jesus had as much
value when it flowed in His veins as when it was shed
upon the cross. They also teach that salvation is by
the life that He lived among men, going about teaching and doing good. This directly denies the Bible
which teaches that man is redeemed by the blood of
Christ, for the blood could be no redemption price,
it could be no ransom paid out, as long as it was in
His veins. Man's unwillingness to confess himself
a sinner is back of this teaching. To do away with
the redemption price is to deny the need of it. To
deny the need of it is to deny sin and the consequences of sin.

His earthly life, as lived by Jesus never has and
never can redeem a single man from the penalty of
the law. It is expressly stated that He was "made

under the law" (Gal. 4:4). That means that Jesus lived on earth subject to God's law, including the Ten Commandments, just the same as any Israelite of His day and before. Therefore, by His perfect life He was Himself saved from the penalty of the law and had access to God, but most certainly no one else has such access by His earthly life.

There is, however, a value to mankind in His perfect earthly life. It is this. By being perfect He did not, as already mentioned, need to die because of sin committed by Himself. He could, therefore, die for others who were sinners and in so doing give His life a ransom for them.

The death of Christ, then, is the very center of salvation. But there are those who will accept this statement and still deny the need for the death of Christ as a redemption price. They say that the death of Jesus is the supreme example of sacrifice for man to behold, and by seeing that and living sacrificial lives men will be saved. This cannot be so, for the Bible nowhere teaches that any moral influence goes out from the cross that causes unsaved men to be good, or even better, and thereby become acceptable to God.

Redeemed From Under Law

When God redeems man from the penalty, or curse, of the law He also redeems him from being under law. As already quoted, "God sent forth His Son . . . to redeem them that were under the law" (Gal. 4:4, 5). It cannot be otherwise for where the penalty is done away the force of the law is also done away. The law is not law without the penalty. From the moment a person is redeemed God does not deal with him on the basis of law, but on an entirely different basis and that is according to grace. ". . . ye are not under law, but under grace" (Rom. 6:14 A.S.V.). The law has nothing more to say. It cannot declare the redeemed person guilty. "There is . . . now no condemnation to them that are in Christ Jesus" (Rom. 8:1 A.S.V.). Redemption, then, results in an entirely different attitude on the part of God toward those who are redeemed.

Redemption Is From Sin and the Power of Sin

When God deals with man on the basis of grace He continues the work of redemption even to the extent of delivering from that for which the law imposed the penalty, namely sin. God's purpose in redeeming man is not only that He might set him free from the penalty of sin but also from sin in his life: "Jesus Christ . . . gave himself for us, that he might redeem us from all iniquity, and purify unto himself a people for his own possession" (Tit. 2:13, 14 A.S.V.).

The apostle Paul said that he was "sold under sin" and that there was a "law of sin" in his body (Rom. 7:14, 23). Jesus said to the Jews, "Everyone that committeth sin is the bondservant of sin" (John 8:34 A.S.V.). Man is surely in bondage under sin. Sin rules in his life but from that also is deliverance. This deliverance is by the power of God and because He acts in grace on behalf of everyone that is delivered from the penalty of sin. "Sin shall not have dominion over you; for ye are not under law but under grace" (Rom. 6:14 A.S.V.). This is so because the law of the Spirit of life in Christ Jesus sets free from the law of sin and death which is inherited from Adam (Rom. 8:2).

Redemption of the Body

The apostle Paul speaks of a still future redemption for which believers are now waiting. "And . . . even we ourselves groan within ourselves, waiting for the adoption, *to wit*, the redemption of our body" (Rom. 8:23).

In the death of Christ there was redemption from the penalty of the broken law and part of that penalty was physical death. Man's body became mortal, subject to death and corruption. In that it became subject to death, it became subject to sickness and disease. Man is afflicted with all kinds of ailments. For these there is healing in the death of Christ, but most emphatically, man has not yet entered into the enjoyment thereof. Paul says, ". . . we ourselves groan within ourselves waiting for . . . the redemption of the body." That day is still in the future. It shall come, when by the trumpet of God, the dead are raised incorruptible and the living believers are changed. Then this corruptible shall take on incorruption and this mortal immortality (1 Cor. 15:51-54) Not until then shall the work of redemption be completed. Then there shall be complete restoration. The effect of Adam's sin shall be entirely removed.

Redemption Is Unto God

Redemption is not only *from* the penalty of the broken law, it is also said to be unto God. ". . . thou wast slain, and hast redeemed us to God by thy blood" (Rev. 5:9) is the song of praise to the Lamb that the redeemed shall sing in heaven.

All who are saved are not their own, they belong to Christ by right of redemption. "What? know ye not that . . . ye are not your own? For ye are bought with a price: therefore glorify God in your body, and in your Spirit, which are God's" (1 Cor. 6:19, 20).

The purpose of redemption, then, is that God might have "a people for his own possession" (Tit. 2:14 A.S.V.).

Redemption Is Eternal

Just one more closing thought about redemption, because Christ is infinite and His blood, the redemption price, is incorruptible, redemption must be eternal and that is what God says of it (Heb. 9:12). Therefore that which God does for the believer because of redemption must stand throughout all eternity.

7

God's Justice Satisfied

IN THE preceding chapter the value of the death of Christ as a ransom price to redeem man from the penalty of the law was seen. Christ's death was seen to be on behalf of man. In this chapter an additional value; a value to God Himself in the death of Christ, is to be considered. Failure to recognize that there is a value to God in the death of Christ is the cause of much misunderstanding and false teaching.

Salvation is a work of God on behalf of man, but in order that He might do this work He had to also do something on behalf of Himself. God in love longed to save man from the consequences of Adam's sin. Even as soon as Adam sinned God came in the cool of the evening and called Adam and said, "Where art thou?" God's loving heart has ever gone out to save fallen man. Few are aware of this important fact.

Bue He Who is love is also infinitely righteous. He is also unchangeable. God's infinite and unchangeable righteousness and justice demanded that the penalty of His law which the creature, man, had broken, must be imposed and the execution of it carried out. God's infinite justice therefore limited His own love. If God was to save man, He had to do something on behalf of Himself so that He could remove the consequences of sin without compromising justice.

And God's love did find a way by which the limitation by justice would be met and removed. "Herein is love, not that we loved God, but that he loved us, and sent his Son *to be* the propitiation for our sins" (1 John 4:10). "And he is the propitiation for our sins: and not for ours only, but also for the sins of the whole world" (1 John 2:2).

To understand the meaning of these verses it is necessary to understand the meaning of the word propitiation. It is "that which . . . appeases [or satisfies] the divine justice and conciliates [or wins over] the divine favor."

The meaning of the above verses, then, is that love is expressed in that God sent His Son to satisfy His own justice and to make it possible for Him to extend favor to man. This expression of love is not only for those who are saved but for all mankind.

It is well to be here reminded of that which constituted the demand of God's justice and how Jesus Christ satisfied that demand. God's justice demanded death because of transgression of His law. "The day that thou eatest thereof thou shalt surely die" (Gen. 2:17). God's love could not remit that penalty. It could not set it aside. God's holy and righteous law must be upheld. His wrath against the unrighteousness of man must take its course.

When the Son of God was sent He came into the world as a man. He lived here thirty-three years as a man and in every detail of His life He satisfied all that God's justice demanded. Then He voluntarily went to the cross. He, the Creator of man, was, by wicked men, nailed to the cross. There sin, as rebellion against God, reached its climax. And when He hung on the cross God laid upon Him the sins of the whole human race. "Jehovah hath laid on him the iniquity of us all" (Isa. 53:6 A.S.V.). That included the first sin by Adam. It also included every sin of every one of the seed of Adam born up to that time and even more, the sins of all men yet to be born. The sins of all were laid upon Him. Then God's judgment upon sin fell upon Him. "And . . . Jesus cried with a loud voice, saying . . . My God, my God, why hast thou forsaken me?" And ". . . when he had cried again with a loud voice, [He] yielded up the ghost" (Matt. 27:46, 50). Here was death because of the sins of mankind. It was a double death; spiritual death because in being forsaken by God He was separated from Him and physical death in yielding up the ghost. And that is exactly the curse that rested upon man because of sin. "But he *was* wounded for our transgressions, *he was* bruised for our iniquities: the chastisement of our peace was upon him" (Isa. 53:5).

The demands of God's justice had been met. The justice of God is no longer a restraining influence to prevent Him from saving those who will come to Him by the only way (John 14:6), even by Jesus Christ, who is the propitiation for our sins.

There is a statement in the Bible that clearly states that God's purpose in sending His Son was on His own behalf. It was that He might remain just and save the sinner. It is found in Paul's great treatise on justification by faith. He there declares that God set forth Christ as a propitiation that God might ". . .

be just, and the justifier of him which believeth in
Jesus" (Rom. 3:25, 26). According to this God could
not remain just and justify any sinner apart from the
fact that the demands of His justice were met by
Jesus Christ when He died on the cross.

Dr. C. I. Scofield in his note on Romans 3:25 calls
attention to the fact that the Greek word which is
there translated "propitiation" is also used in Hebrews 9:5 where it is translated "mercy seat." The
cross then, where propitiation was made, because
judgment was passed upon sin, became the place
where God shows mercy. That is the essential meaning of the cross of Christ. He who will come to the
cross as the place where his own sins have been
judged in the person of Christ will receive mercy at
the hand of God. Because of the cross, grace becomes
sovereign and reigns unto eternal life (Rom. 5:21).

Throughout the ages of human existence man has
realized that there is a wrath of God that needs to
be appeased before man can come unto Him, but
relatively few, indeed very few, know that God
Himself has provided a propitiation. After Adam
had sinned he hid, because, as he said, "I was afraid"
(Gen. 3:10). Ever since then there has been in the
heart of man a fear to meet God because of His sup-
posed wrath toward man. Mythology is filled with
stories of men trying to appease their gods. So also
the heathen go to great excesses trying to appease
their gods. And the feeling that something is demanded of man to satisfy the vengeance of God is far
from lacking in even so-called Christian lands. Every

thought of man that something can be done to lessen his punishment in the hereafter is a confession that he feels that the wrath of God needs to be appeased and that God is not favorably inclined unto him.

The central truth of the Gospel, the good news, of the grace of God, and that which is so little understood, it that the wrath of God against all unrighteousness of man has been appeased in the death of His own Son. His justice has been satisfied and now God, in love, is longing to extend pardon and peace to all who will come to Him by the way of the Cross.

8

Clothed in the Righteousness of God

IN CHAPTER VII it was seen that because Jesus Christ was set forth as a propitiation for sin God can be just and justify the one who believes in Jesus. It is important then to consider what it is that God does in justifying man.

The word in the original text translated "justify" is also translated "righteousness." Justification must therefore be related to righteousness and so it is. Justification is the act. Righteousness is the result.

In order that man may come into the presence of God he must have an absolutely righteous standing in His sight. Any unrighteousness that is charged against a man will keep him from seeing God. When God justifies a person He provides that person with the necessary righteous standing before Himself.

Justification is more than pardon and forgiveness of sin. Pardon is negative. It considers the penalty due to transgression. Justification is positive. It gives to man a meritorious standing.

The difference between pardon and justification is excellently illustrated by the events connected with a racial and military plot which stirred the whole world a few decades ago. This illustration has been used by others, but is well worth repeating.

A Jewish soldier named Alfred Dreyfus showed such marked ability that in 1891 he was appointed to the general staff of the French Army. Three years later he was arrested, being charged with selling military information to Germany. His trial resulted in dismissal from the army, public degradation and commitment to the French penal colony on Devil's Island. Due to popular demand Dreyfus was retried in 1899, but was again declared guilty. Because of public dissatisfaction with the result of the trial the President of France pardoned Dreyfus. But the friends of Dreyfus were not satisfied with a mere pardon and in 1906 in a third trial Dreyfus was completely vindicated. He was given the more advanced rank of major and enrolled in the Legion of Honor.

When Alfred Dreyfus was pardoned after the second trial the penalty of the crime of which he was accused was remitted. He was taken from the penal colony on Devil's Island. He came back to his family and friends, but the stigma of being a traitor rested upon him. But when, through the third trial he became vindicated and was promoted to the rank of major and enrolled in the Legion of Honor, he was justified before the whole world. He had a standing of perfect righteousness and in addition thereto was given recognition that comes only to those who have served and brought honor to their country.

This is exactly what happens when God justifies the one who believes in Jesus. The only difference is that Alfred Dreyfus, an innocent man, was falsely accused and convicted, while the one whom God justifies is a truly guilty sinner, and deserves the penalty that the law imposes.

All Trespasses Forgiven

Because man is a sinner and is guilty, it is necessary for God, in justifying a person, first to pardon and forgive his sins.

God's forgiveness in saving a person is said to be the forgiveness of "all trespasses" (Col. 2:13). This forgiveness of trespasses is not the same as God's forgiveness of the child's sins against Himself as the Father (1 John 1:7-9). It is a judicial forgiveness by which the sinner is declared to be free from all trespasses. It is done once and for all when the sinner comes to the cross.

God never treats sin lightly. His forgiveness is not a mere act of leniency in remitting or setting aside the penalty as when one man forgives another. God forgives only because the penalty has been paid by Another, even by Jesus Christ. "For Christ also hath once suffered for sins, the just for the unjust, that he might bring us to God" (1 Pet. 3:18). Because ". . . without the shedding of blood is no remission," God's forgiveness demands redemption.

For Christ's Sake

Forgiveness by God is said to be "for Christ's sake" (Eph. 4:32). It involves therefore the justice of God. Because Christ died and thereby paid the penalty for sin, it would be unrighteous of God not to forgive the one who accepts Jesus Christ as the propitiation for his sins. If an earthly judge imposed a prison term or an alternate fine and a third party paid that fine, it would be unjust after the penalty had been paid, to imprison the one who had been found guilty.

According to Riches of His Grace

Though God's forgiveness involves His justice it is also said to be according to the riches of His grace (Eph. 1:7). This is so because it was the love of God that sent His Son into the world (John 3:16) and it was by the grace of God that He tasted death for every man (Heb. 2:9). Notice, it is not only according to grace but the "riches of His grace." There is no stinted forgiveness by God. It is both free and full.

The completeness of the forgiveness in this age is seen in comparison with the forgiveness of the sins of the Old Testament saints. In the Old Testament days forgiveness was acomplished by removing the sin from the sinner (Ps. 103:12). The sacrifices of the Old Testament were for an *atonement* for sin. To atone for sin means to cover, but not to entirely do away with it. By those sacrifices, they that brought them could not be made perfect. By them was a yearly reminder of sin. "For *it is* not possible that the blood of bulls and goats should take away sin" (Heb. 10:4). But the Lamb of God takes away sin (John 1:29) and those who are sanctified once for all by that sacrifice are perfected forever (Heb. 10:10, 14). This is a complete and unalterable judicial forgiveness of sin which gives to the believer a standing before God as perfect as though he had never sinned.

This is beautifully illustrated by an incident that
happened many years ago. A newly married couple
had invited members of their two families to a Sunday
dinner. The guests were seated around the table. All
desired to be at their best. As the rich brown gravy
was being passed one young lady accidently tipped
the bowl with a resultant large brown spot on the
immaculately clean and shining linen tablecloth. The
hostess quickly and skillfully scraped up the gravy and
spread a napkin over the spot and the meal went on.
The napkin did not take away the spot; it merely covered it so that the dinner could go on. To the unfor-
tunate young woman who had spilled the gravy the
white napkin was a constant reminder of her acci-
dent. So the Old Testament sacrifices covered the
sins of the Israelites but were a constant reminder of
sin. The day after the dinner the tablecloth was
washed and the spot taken away. So by the sacrifice
of Christ, believers are washed from their sins in His
blood (Rev. 1: 5). There is no napkin to remind of sin.

From this it is clear that when God deals with the
sin problem of the unsaved one He does not ask him
to put away his sins and live right in the future. That
is impossible for anyone to do and besides that there
would still be unsolved the whole problem of past
sins. No, God judicially and completely forgives
every sin because Christ has paid the penalty for
those sins. What God asks the unsaved to do is to confess that he is a sinner and accept Jesus Christ as having borne the penalty for his sins. That is all anyone
can do to receive God's judicial forgiveness.

Man's Effort to Justify Himself

In all ages man has tried to justify himself before God. He has tried to produce a righteousness which is acceptable to God. When man does so it becomes self-righteousness and not a God-provided righteousness. Self-righteousness does not, in fact cannot, save any man. The Israelites of Paul's time went about to establish their own righteousness. They even had "zeal for God" (Rom. 10:1-3) but they were not saved because of that. These people were very religious. They fasted and said long prayers. They observed all religious holidays and carried on the temple worship. The reason they were not saved was that in all they did, they were trying to establish their own righteousness and that was not acceptable to God.

So today man tries to establish a righteousness that he thinks should be acceptable to God. He tries to follow Jesus' example and to obey the Sermon on the Mount. He does the best he can to live up to the dictates of his own conscience. Some join the church, become baptized, say prayers and take part in all kinds of religious and philanthropic work. While these things do have their place, the doing of them can in no way add to the righteousness demanded by God of man in order to come into His presence.

Some seem to think that God keeps books with them, charging them with all evil deeds and crediting all good deeds to their account. If the good deeds out-weigh the evil ones they think that they are acceptable to God. This cannot be God's method because He demands perfection in all deeds. It is not a question of a high batting average. It means striking the first pitched ball every time one comes up to bat each day of one's life from the cradle to the grave.

Concerning all self-righteousness the prophet Isaiah said: ". . . all our righteousnesses are as filthy rags" (Isa. 64:6). It has been said that the "filthy rags" here referred to were those worn by lepers and therefore full of leprosy. As leprosy is typical of sin, the picture is perfect, for all of man's self-righteousness is contaminated by sin. All is done in dependence upon self instead of upon God and that, as has been seen, is the essence of sin.

There are some who think that because the law, especially the Ten Commandments, was given by God, the observance of it will give to man a righteous standing before God. That is impossible because God requires absolute obedience and perfection and man cannot render such obedience. "For whosoever shall keep the whole law, and yet offend in one *point*, he is guilty of all" (Jas. 2:10). Because of this ". . . by the deeds of the law there shall no flesh be justified in his [God's] sight" (Rom. 3:20. See also Gal. 2:16).

For four thousand years man had proved himself incapable of being righteous. Both Jews and Gentiles had been proved to be under sin. There was none righteous to be found, no, not one (Rom. 3:9, 10). By the law every mouth was stopped before God (Rom. 3:19). God's law demanded righteousnes by man, but man had failed.

The Righteousness That God Demands
He Also Provides

No man begotten of Adam has lived a perfectly righteous life; one that will for him gain admission into the presence of God. "All have sinned and come short of the glory of God" (Rom. 3:23). But that perfect righteousness that God demands of those who are to come into His presence He also provides. He will Himself clothe with righteousness, as with a garment, all who will accept His righteousness as a free gift.

While none of Adam's seed has been able to live a life of righteousness acceptable to God, when the Son of God came to this earth and became a true man and so lived, He fulfilled every jot and tittle of God's law, (Matt. 5:17, 18), and thus revealed a righteousness acceptable to God.

That the earthly life of Jesus was acceptable to God cannot be questioned. Near the close of it, Jesus took three of His disciples with Him up into a high mountain and was transfigured before them. Moses appeared also with Him as the representative of the law, and Elias as that of the prophets. With these two as witnesses, God spoke out of the cloud saying, "This is my beloved Son in whom I am well pleased." (See Matt. 17:1-5.) This was a clear declaration of God's acceptance of the earthly life of Jesus. Here was One Who had not sinned and come short of the glory of God. He was altogether righteous and was so witnessed by the law and by the prophets.

When the whole world stood guilty before God
and it had been demonstrated that no man could be
justified by his own good works, then God, in the
person of His Son living on this earth as a man, revealed a righteousness acceptable to Himself. This
righteousness is now offered unto all as a gift and it
is clothed as a garment (Isa. 61:10) upon all that believe. This is the message of Romans 3:19-22.

By Grace and Not of Works

The Bible expressly declares that no man can earn
this righteousness by anything whatsoever that he
might do. It is said that is is reckoned to the account
of all that believe in Jesus Christ and that only because of their faith. "Therefore we conclude that a
man is justified by faith without the deeds of the law"
(Rom. 3:28). "But to him that worketh not, but believeth on him that justifieth the ungodly, his faith
is counted for righteousness" (Rom. 4:5. See also Gal.
2:16, 3:8, 24. Read Rom. chapter 4.) Man is therefore
justified freely by the grace of God (Rom. 3:24).

Through Redemption in Christ Jesus

Justification is made possible through the redemption that is in Christ Jesus (Rom. 3:24). It is because
He was set forth as a propitiation for sin, already explained, that God can righteously forgive the sinner
and reckon unto him Christ's perfect righteousness.
When God counted man's sin to Jesus Christ, He
became so thoroughly indentified therewith that He
was actually made sin and died as a sinner. When God

counts righteousness to the believer he becomes so thoroughly identified therewith that he actually becomes the righteousness of God and lives. "Him who knew no sin he [God] made *to be* sin on our behalf; that we might become the righteousnes of God in him" (2 Cor. 5:21 A.S.V.). Only a divinely prepared and perfect righteousness will admit man into the presence of God. No faulty man-made righteousness will do. Therefore it is only because God counts the righteousness of Christ to the one who believes that any man can gain entrance into heaven.

There is no St. Peter at the gate of heaven asking people what good they have done to enter therein. The righteousness of God, which is Christ, is man's only passport to heaven but one who has received that passport is certain to enter therein because nothing can ever be charged against such a one. "Who shall lay anything to the charge of God's elect? *It is* God that justifieth" (Rom. 8:33).

Justification, then, is the imputation of the righteousness of Christ to the one who believes on Him. It is counting to him the merits of Christ. It gives to the believer a perfectly righteous standing before God as perfect as that of Jesus Christ and is apart from any merit on man's part. Justification is demanded by God's holiness and supplied by His love.

The Bible gives a perfect illustration of justification. It is recorded in Genesis 3:21 in these words, "Unto Adam also and to his wife did the Lord God make coats of skins, and clothed them." Adam and his wife had sinned. They stood naked before God and under the judgment of the broken law. By slaying innocent animals, God prepared coats of skins and these He put upon Adam and his wife. By these garments they were made fit for the presence of God. Notice that God made the coats. Adam and his wife did not help in any way. God clothed them. They did not even put the coats on. They gave nothing to God for the coats. The provision of the coats necessitated the death of an innocent third party.

These coats were provided only after Adam had named his wife Eve, because she was the mother of all living. By so doing, Adam (under the judgment of death) showed his faith in God's promise that the woman's seed (Jesus) should destroy the head, or power, of the serpent which is Satan. (See Gen. 3:15, 20.)

Herein are all the elements of justification. God prepares a garment of righteousness and in it He clothes all who believe in Jesus Christ as the One who delivers from sin. Man can give nothing in return for this garment nor can he put it on himself. The provision of righteousness is made possible only by the death of an innocent, a sinless, third Person, even Jesus Christ.

9

Brought Into Harmony with God

IN SINNING, as previously pointed out, the first man listened to the tempter. He yielded himself to the influence and power of Satan and so mankind became subject to his power. Because of this condition, God in saving man must deliver him from the power of darkness. Furthermore, it was seen that, in sinning, man violated God's law, became guilty and came under the sentence of death. It was therefore also necessary for God to redeem him from the curse of the law and from under the law.

There is one more thing that happened when man sinned. In considering the subject of sin it was seen that because God *created* man, all that man was and all that he had came from God. Therefore, man's proper attitude toward God was one of complete dependence upon Him. Man's sin consisted in a declaration of independence of God and dependence upon self. This attitude taken by man was nothing less than a rebellion against God and His sovereignty, or government, over man, including His provision for man. When any group of people declares its independence of a government under which they have lived, it is a rebellion. If and when they are able to establish their independence and exist as a separate government then their action partakes of the nature of a revolution. Man has never been able to establish an independent existence apart from God. There are some who think and act as though they can do this very thing, but as long as man cannot exist without God's sunshine, His air and His rain, man cannot claim to be independent of God. All independence of God by man, then, is and must be in the nature of a rebellion against Him. The rebel human race was in need of reconciliation.

In listening to the tempter's words, as has already been said, man became subject to him. Thus man became alienated from God and an enemy to Him. Here also was need for reconciliation.

After Adam and his wife had sinned ". . . they heard the voice of Jehovah God walking in the garden in the cool of the day: and the man and his wife hid themselves from the presence of Jehovah God amongst the trees of the garden. And Jehovah God called unto the man, and said unto him, Where *art* thou? And he said, I heard thy voice in the garden, and I was afraid because I was naked; and I hid myself" (Gen. 3:8-10 A.S.V.).

A change had taken place within Adam. He had become estranged from God. He had alienated himself from Him. Fear of God had taken the place of love, confidence and trust. Instead of drawing near to God he drew away from Him. By his sin Adam became far off from God. Friendship with God with accompanying communion, companionship, fellowship and intimacy were lost and replaced by enmity and estrangement.

As Adam passed his sinful nature onto his posterity so also with it he passed along the state of alienation from God and the feeling of fear of Him.

One need not go far to find evidence that mankind is still in that estranged relationship to God. The evidence of man's fear for God can be multiplied a thousand-fold. Every effort on the part of man to appease God and every effort to do something to gain God's favor is a witness to man's alienation from Him. Every fear of death and a judgment to come testifies to the broken harmony between God and man.

This state of alienation of all men from God requires a special work on the part of God on behalf of man. Redemption from under the law and from the penalty of the broken law made it possible for God to justify man so that in the sight of His law man was counted as perfectly righteous. But to be right with God on a strictly legal basis does not necessarily mean to be on intimate terms with Him.

If one of two persons who are very friendly with each other commits some illegal act whereby he harms his friend, it is possible that the legal aspect of the act be settled without bringing the two back into a state of friendship. They may forever remain alienated from each other. In addition to a legal settlement there must be brought about a reconciliation between them. So also, even though man has been redeemed from the penalty of the law and is reckoned as perfectly righteous in the sight of the law, he also needs to be reconciled to God as a part of God's work of restoring that which was lost to man by Adam's sin. Reconciliation, then, is an important part of salvation.

God's work of reconciliation is a work on behalf

of man. When two men are to be reconciled to each other it is possible, in fact probable, that there is something wrong in each that needs to be corrected. They are reconciled to each other. Not so in the case of reconciliation of man to God. Man is out of harmony with God and only he needs to be reconciled. "God was in Christ [on the cross] reconciling the world [mankind] unto himself" (2 Cor. 5:19).

To reconcile means to cause to be friendly again; to restore to friendship; to bring back to harmony; to cause to be no longer at variance. It was man that broke the friendship with God. Man, by sinning, became a discordant note in God's universe. That which is in man that brought about the discord and the alienation from God must be dealt with. And that is just what God does in reconciling man to Himself, for "God was in Christ reconciling the world unto himself, not imputing their trespasses unto them" (2 Cor. 5:19).

In justification, which is because of redemption, man's trespasses are considered as a violation of God's law and are forgiven because Jesus Christ paid the penalty on the cross and man is restored to a righteous standing before God's law. In reconciliation God deals with the trespasses of man as that which expressed man's rebellion against His authority, in fact, against His government, including His provision for man.

That which caused man to fear God, to hide from Him, to be at enmity with Him and out of harmony with Him, is not counted against man. That which constituted rebellion is considered as though it had not taken place.

The awfulness of the separation and alienation of man from God by sin is best understood by considering the cost at which God brought about reconciliation. It was by nothing less than the death of the Son of God. It is said that ". . . when we were enemies, we were reconciled to God by the death of his Son" (Rom. 5:10). Again, "And you, that were sometimes alienated and enemies in *your* mind by wicked works, yet now hath he reconciled in the body of His flesh, through death" (Col. 1:21, 22).

The penalty for rebellion against a human government is death. That was well-known by Benjamin Franklin when he said, "We must all hang together, or assuredly we shall all hang separately." So also the penalty for rebellion against God is death. Therefore when Christ died on the cross to reconcile man to God He died there in man's place as a rebel.

When the Jewish leaders brought Jesus before Pilate they charged that He had been found perverting the nation, forbidding to give tribute to Caesar, and saying that He was king (Luke 23:1, 2). All of these are acts of sedition, or rebellion, and it was on these charges that Jesus was tried. Pilate after having examined Jesus said to the Jews, "I, having examined *him* before you, found no fault in this man touching those things whereof ye accuse him: No, nor yet Herod: for he sent him back unto us and, behold, nothing worthy of death hath been done by him. I will therefore chastise him, and release him. But they cried out all together, saying, Away with this man, and release unto us Barabbas:—one who for a certain insurrection made in the city, and for murder was cast into prison. . . . And Pilate gave sentence that what they asked for should be done. And he released him that for insurrection and murder had been cast into prison" (Luke 23:14-19, 24, 25 A.S.V.). He who had not committed rebellion died as a rebel and he who had committed rebellion was set free and that only because Jesus died. Had Jesus not died, Barabbas would have been crucified. But Barabbas was not alone in gaining his freedom through the death of Jesus. Jesus, by the grace of God, tasted death for every man (Heb. 2:9) and that was in order that the creature, man, who had made insurrection against God, might become reconciled to Him.

Sometimes men are called upon to make their peace with God. There is nothing in the Bible on which to base that appeal. In fact it contradicts the statements that "he [Christ] is our peace" and that He in His flesh has abolished the enmity and so made peace (Eph. 2:14, 15). Man cannot make his peace with God, all he can do is to accept the peace that has been made on his behalf by Jesus Christ on the cross and which is freely offered by God. Reconciliation is a work of God and of Him alone.

Through reconciliation man enters from a state of enmity against God into a state of peace with Him. When the Son of God was born as a babe in Bethlehem, the angels proclaimed, "on earth peace" (Luke

2:14). This meant that He who was then born should reconcile man to God.

Those who have become reconciled to God instead of being far off are made nigh to God. They have access by the Spirit to the Father. The feeling of fear for God is replaced with one of love and confidence in Him. They are "no more strangers and foreigners, but fellow citizens with the saints, and of the household of God" (Eph. 2:19). To be of the household of God means that all the goodness and omnipotence of God is available unto them.

Though man cannot make his peace with God he must by an act of his will accept the peace that Jesus Christ has made for him. God, through the death of Jesus Christ, removed that which caused the enmity and alienation, but each individual person must change his own attitude toward God. He cannot maintain his rebellious attitude and become reconciled to God. Paul, the apostle, said, ". . . we are ambassadors for Christ, as though God did beseech *you* by us: we pray *you* in Christ's stead, be ye reconciled to God" (2 Cor. 5:20). Only as man is willing to surrender his dependence upon himself and his independence of God can he become reconciled to God.

10

A New Life With a New Nature

IN SALVATION God does more than deliver man from the power of darkness, redeem him from the penalty of the law and reconcile him unto Himself. All this can be done for man and, though great as it is, it does no more than restore to man that which was lost by Adam's sin. In addition to this God makes of man a new and infinitely higher being than Adam ever was. This is accomplished by regeneration, or by being born again.

A man of the Pharisees named Nicodemus came to Jesus one night and said to Him, "Rabbi, we know that thou art a teacher come from God: for no man can do these miracles that thou doest, except God be with him" (John 3:2).

It is well to consider the type of person Nicodemus was. He is spoken of as a man, a descendant of Adam. As such he possessed Adam's fallen human nature. He was a Jew, one of God's chosen people. He was a Pharisee, one of the strictest religious sect of the Jews who were separated unto legal self-righteousness. He was a ruler of the Jews, therefore a member of their council, the Sanhedrin. He was the teacher of Israel. To him others looked as to a guide in matters pertaining to God. He was one who had earnestly endeavored to fulfill the requirements of the greatest moral code the world has ever known, the Ten Commandments and the Mosaic ordinances. Evidently in him was found the highest type of manhood possible under the Mosaic law and in fact, any other moral code under which man has lived.

Unquestionably Nicodemus lived up to the light that he had. He constantly sought more and so, as one who desired to learn better how to live a life pleasing to God, he came to Jesus to learn of Him. In Him Nicodemus saw a teacher come direct from God.

To understand the exact attitude of Nicodemus to Jesus it is necessary to consider just what any teacher can do for the one who comes to him to learn. All that a teacher can do is to instruct. The learning must be by the student himself. The improvement in the life of the student comes from the development of his latent talents. These are stimulated by the teacher but no talents can be contributed by the teacher that are not already in the student. To whatever degree the life of a student can be developed it must necessarily remain the same life as it was at the beginning. In coming to Jesus as to a teacher, Nicodemus hoped to learn how to develop and improve his life so that it would be pleasing to God. He had all his life been reading the law as a guide to righteous living, now he came to Jesus in the same attitude.

It was to this attitude of desiring to improve himself that Jesus *answered* Nicodemus and said; "Verily, verily, I say unto thee, Except a man be born again, he cannot see the kingdom of God" (John 3:3). Jesus' answer to Nicodemus is the answer of the Son of God to man's desire to establish his own righteousness and

by his own goodness gain entrance into the kingdom
of God. By this one answer, made to one of the most
religious, punctilious, educated, honored and truth-
seeking men of his generation, Jesus declared that
natural man, however refined, moral and educated he
might become, cannot thereby gain entrance into the
kingdom of God and His heaven. There is not that in
man which can be developed into a life acceptable to
God. How this with one stroke sets aside all present
day teaching that Jesus was the greatest teacher the
world has ever known and that by following His
teachings one can be saved! While the *saved person*
should carefully consider the teachings of Jesus
[though some of them were for the Jewish nation
alone] the unsaved person may all his life strive to follow these teachings and still at the end of his life find
heaven's door closed to him. Jesus said, "Except a man
be born again, he cannot see the kingdom of God."

The word birth, when used literally, always means
the coming into existence of a new life. This life *always* partakes of the nature of the parents. When a
wolf, or a sheep, is born there is a new life which has
the wolf or sheep nature, as the case may be. When a
child is born into the world, a new life comes into
existence. This life has a human nature which, as has
already been shown (See page 35), is sinful. It is
shapen in iniquity and conceived in sin (Ps. 51:5).
Such a life cannot change its nature. The prophet
Jeremiah wrote, "Can the Ethiopian change his skin,
or the leopard his spots? *then* may ye also do good,
that are accustomed to do evil" (Jer. 13:23). Nor can

it be said that in such a life there is a divine spark
that needs but to be stirred to bring that life into
fellowship with God.

Jesus explained that to be born again is to "be
born of water and *of* the Spirit" (John 3:5). This
statement is illuminated by a verse in Paul's letter to
Titus, "Not by works of righteousness which we
have done, but according to his mercy he saved us, by
the washing of regeneration, and renewing of the
Holy Ghost (Tit. 3:5). To be "born of water" is
"the washing of regeneration." It is a cleansing of
the individual from sin "with the washing of water
by the word" (Eph. 5:26). Jesus said to his disciples,
"Now ye are clean through the word which I have
spoken unto you" (John 15:3).

To be born of the Spirit is to be born "not of blood,
nor of the will of the flesh, nor of the will of man, but
of God" (John 1:13). It is to be "born again, not of
corruptible seed, but of incorruptible, by the word of
God, which liveth and abideth for ever" (1 Pet. 1:23).

By the new birth, God becomes Father of those so
born and they are called His children (1 John 3:1)
but apart from regeneration there is no fatherhood
of God for man in this age.

With the new birth there is also a new nature. It
is the nature of God, the One by Whom life is given.
As the life of one born of the flesh is mortal because
Adam became mortal, so the life of one born of God
is eternal because God's life is eternal. This eternal
life is the present possession of all who are born
again (John 5:24). One who is born again cannot die.

As the old life, born of the flesh, has a sinful nature, so the new life born of God has His divine (2 Pet. 1:4) and sinless nature. "Whosoever is born of God doth not commit sin; for his seed remaineth in him: and he cannot sin, because he is born of God" (1 John 3:9). This new life is not a development of a "divine spark" in the natural man; it is a new and entirely distinct life from God, just as the natural life is from the earthly parents.

Jesus made it very clear to Nicodemus that the new birth and the old natural, or physical, birth are separate and distinct. He said, "That which is born of the flesh is flesh; and that which is born of the Spirit is spirit" (John 3:6). The two have nothing in common, in fact they are in conflict with each other. "For the flesh lusteth against the Spirit, and the Spirit against the flesh: and these are contrary the one to the other" (Gal. 5:17). "For they that are after the flesh do mind the things of the flesh; but they that are after the Spirit the things of the Spirit. For to be carnally minded *is* death; but to be spiritually minded *is* life and peace. Because the carnal mind [i.e. the mind of natural man] *is* enmity against God: for it is not subject to the law of God, neither indeed can be" (Rom. 8:5-7). "The natural man receiveth not the things of the Spirit of God: for they are foolishness unto him: neither can he know *them* because they are spiritually discerned" (1 Cor. 2:14).

From the above it is evident that it is impossible by education, culture or reformation to change the natural state of man into the spiritual state of the kingdom of God.

The new birth, then, is God's answer to that phase or aspect of the sin problem which involves the sinful nature of man. In salvation God gives to man through spiritual birth a new sinless nature like unto His Own.

But how about the old sinful nature of those who are saved? What becomes of that? It still lives on in the individual as long as that person lives in the present mortal body. When at death, the spirit of the saved departs from his body then the old nature dies.

It is because the old sinful nature survives that those who have been saved can and do commit sin. This happens when, in the conflict between the carnal and spiritual, the carnal gains the upper hand. God's appeal to all who are saved is to "Mortify [put to death] therefore your members which are upon the earth" (Col. 3:5) and "Reckon ye also yourselves to be dead indeed unto sin, but alive unto God through Jesus Christ our Lord" (Rom. 6:11).

The New Creation in Christ Jesus

The one who is "born again" is "created in Christ Jesus" (Eph. 2:10). "In Christ Jesus neither circumcision [i.e. Jews] availeth anything, nor uncircumcision [i.e. Gentiles], but a new creation" (Gal. 6:15). This creation takes the place of the old creation in Adam. "If any man be in Christ he is a new creature: old things are passed away; behold, all things are become new" (2 Cor. 5:17). This new creation is "the

new man, which after God is created in righteousness and true holiness" (Eph. 4:24).

It is not difficult to understand that the angelic
host, made up of created beings, belongs to a creation
entirely distinct from man. There is even a greater
difference between mankind as descended from Adam
and the new creation in Christ Jesus, for that new
creation is even higher than the angels. It is important
to recognize that the one who is born again belongs
to this higher order of spiritual beings. It is difficult
to do so as long as the new life dwells in the present
mortal bodies of the old creation in Adam. In them
there is still much evidence of the old or first creation.

It was seen that the first creation derived its sinful
nature from its federal head Adam. By his sin all
became sinners and as the penalty for that sin was
death, so death passed upon all men. "Wherefore, as
by one man sin entered into the world [mankind],
and death by sin; and so death passed upon all men"
(Rom. 5:12).

The words which are written large over the first
creation, that of which Adam is the federal head, are
SIN HATH REIGNED UNTO DEATH. That condition is
unalterable, for God had commanded Adam not to
eat of the fruit of the tree of knowledge of good and
evil and had made death the penalty for disobedience. This meant death in its fullest significance,
physical death, spiritual death and the second death
which is the final everlasting separation of the body,
soul and spirit from God. God's commandment had
been broken and the penalty could not be avoided.

When the Son of God became flesh and came into
the world, He dwelt among men of the old creation.
But He was not of it. He was not of the seed of
Adam, but of the seed of the woman. He was con-
ceived by the Holy Ghost. Therefore, He did not
possess Adam's sinful nature. He was full of truth
(John 1:14). He was in the *likeness* of sinful flesh
(Rom. 8:3), but no sin was in Him.

Then through infinite love, He identified Himself
with the first creation and took upon Himself the
guilt thereof. He was the Lamb of God which taketh
away the sin of the world. As a result, He tasted
death for every man (Heb. 2:9). Even with Him, sin
assayed to triumph unto death.

But God raised Him up, "having loosed the pains
of death: because it was not possible that he should
be holden of it" (Acts 2:24). He arose victorious over
death. The Son of God? Yes, but also the Son of man.
With His resurrection there was a new creation raised
by God out of the death of the old. All who are saved
are quickened together with Christ in this resurrection. "But God . . . even when we were dead in
sins, hath quickened us together with Christ, (by
grace ye are saved;) and hath raised *us* up together,
and made *us* sit together in heavenly *places* in Christ
Jesus" (Eph. 2:4-6).

As the first creation has one man as its federal
head, so also has the new creation the man Jesus
Christ (Rom. 5:15). The first creation received its
sinful nature from its federal head, Adam. The new
creation received its righteous nature from its fed-

eral head, the man Jesus Christ, for "by the obedience of One, shall many be made righteous" (Rom.
5:19). *In each case, the nature of the creation depends upon the act of the head. It does not depend
upon the acts of those who issue from those heads.*

As the unalterable law of the first is SIN UNTO DEATH,
so the law of the new is GRACE REIGNS THROUGH
RIGHTEOUSNESS UNTO ETERNAL LIFE. This law of the
new creation is even more unalterable than that of
the first creation: "For if by one man's offence death
reigned by one; much more they which receive abundance of grace and of the gift of righteousness shall
reign in life by One Jesus Christ" (Rom. 5:17). Since
the head cannot be condemned (Rom. 6:9, 10), the
members of the new creation cannot be condemned.

Salvation, then, includes something vastly more
than a restoration of man to the original perfect condition in which he was when created. It includes a
new eternal life having a divine nature. This new
life becomes the immediate possession of the one
who believes in Jesus Christ. All who are so "born
again" become a part of the new and infinitely perfect and righteous creation in Christ Jesus.

11

Saved By His Life

PAUL writing to the Christians in Rome said, "For if, when we were enemies, we were reconciled to God by the death of his Son, much more, being reconciled, we shall be saved by his life" (Rom. 5:10). Notice the two words, "much more." It is great that all who have believed on Jesus Christ are reconciled to God by the death of His Son. But it is a far greater thing that all who have been so reconciled shall be saved by the life of the Son of God.

This does not mean that they are saved by the earthly life of Jesus and by following His example. The life here referred to is the present life of Jesus Christ at the right hand of God in heaven. That this is so is taught clearly by the following passage; "But this *man* [Jesus] because he continueth ever . . . is able also to save them to the uttermost that come unto God by him, seeing he ever liveth to make intercession for them" (Heb. 7:24, 25).

The simple meaning of all this is that after Jesus Christ died on the cross to set men free from the power of Satan, to redeem them from the penalty of the law and to reconcile them unto God, He arose from the grave and ascended into heaven where He now is in the presence of God the Father. His work there is to see to it that all who come to God by Him [i.e. His death] shall be saved from wrath and brought into eternal glory in the presence of God where He now is. This salvation is said to be to the uttermost.

Because it is conditioned upon His continuing forever it must be a continuing salvation, one that cannot be terminated. Here as always, salvation is represented as an unfailing work of God.

Just how those who have become reconciled to God by the death of His Son are saved by His life is learned from the expression, ". . . he ever liveth to make intercession for them." In other words, because the Son of man intercedes with the all-powerful Father on behalf of those who come unto God by Him, God will exercise His power on their behalf.

It is helpful to consider the nature of this intercession of Jesus Christ with the Father. Instances of His intercession for His disciples while with them on earth give some idea of how at the right hand of God He now prays for all believers.

Just before the betrayal and arrest of Jesus by the Jews, He said to Peter, "Simon, Simon, behold, Satan hath desired *to have* you, that he may sift *you* as wheat: but I have prayed for thee, that thy faith fail not . . ." (Luke 22:31, 32). Bible readers are familiar with the story (Mark 14:54, 66-72) how after Jesus had spoken these words Peter did deny Him three times. Did Jesus' prayer for Peter go unanswered? It did not. Jesus did not pray that Peter should not be tempted. Neither did He pray that Peter should not fail and deny Him. No, He prayed that Peter's faith should not fail. And Peter's faith did not fail. Though he sinned against his Lord by denying Him, even to the point of cursing, his faith failed not. He was restored and in his later life he was seen with an even stronger faith than before. So Jesus now prays for those who come unto God by Him that their faith fail not.

There is another example of the Lord's intercession for His Own. It is found in the seventeenth chapter of John's Gospel. This whole chapter has been called Christ's intercessory prayer. Jesus makes it clear that this prayer is not for the world (that is, all mankind), but only for those whom the Father had given to Him out of the world (v. 9). This was all who believed on Him as the Son of God. But it was for many more than those who were then living. It was not for them alone, "but for them also which shall believe on me through their word" (v. 20). This prayer, then, was for all who throughout the centuries since, even down to this time, have believed the gospel message and accepted Jesus Christ as their Saviour.

What then did He pray on behalf of all believers of this age? His first prayer for them was, "Holy Father, keep through thine own name those whom thou hast given me" (v. 11). His first concern for those for whom He died and who become reconciled to God by His death was that they be kept safe. That is even now His concern for those who come unto God by Him. They shall be saved to the uttermost.

Is there any possibility that this intercession by Jesus with the Father shall go unanswered? To say so would be to say that God fails to answer the petitions of His Own Son.

Then Jesus enlarged upon His prayer on behalf of

His own. He said, "I pray not that thou shouldest
take them out of the world, but that thou shouldest
keep them from the evil" (v. 15). It was a greater
prayer that they be kept from evil in an evil world
than that they be taken out of it so as to be kept from
being lost. If there had been any question about the
greater petition being fulfilled, surely He would
have asked for the lesser. Therefore all who are His
Own because of His intercession are being kept from
the evil while in this world. This does not mean that
they do not fail at times as did Peter, but that the
evil shall not overcome them.

He further prayed, "that they all [all the saved of
this age] may be one; as thou, Father, *art* in me, and
I in thee, that they also may be one in us" (v. 21).
This is a prayer that all believers may come into that
perfect unity (more than harmony) with God the
Father and God the Son as exists between them.
No finite mind can grasp the implications of this
prayer but it is nothing less than a divine position
for those who believe on the Son of God.

Again He prayed, "Father, I will that they also,
whom thou hast given me, be with me where I am;
that they may behold my glory, which thou hast
given me" (v. 24).

All of this is a part of His intercession for His own
and all is a part of being saved by His life.

But there is another aspect to the intercession of
Christ for His Own. His intercession may partake of
the nature of the pleadings of a lawyer before a court
of justice. There are times when one who has been

saved commits sin. When that happens there is one who now has access to heaven (Job 1:6) that brings accusations against the sinning child of God. He is Satan, who is called the "accuser of our brethren" and is said to accuse "them before our God day and night" (Rev. 12:10). This condition calls for intercession by Him Who is at the right hand of God. But the accuser (the prosecuting attorney) can lay nothing to the charge of those for whom Christ intercedes. It is written, "Who shall lay anything to the charge of God's elect? *It is* God that justifieth. Who *is* he that condemneth? *It is* Christ that died, yea rather, that is risen again, who is even at the right hand of God, who also maketh intercession for us" (Rom. 8:33, 34).

There is another passage that presents the same truth. "My little children [those born of God], these things write I unto you, that ye sin not. And if any man sin, we have an advocate with the Father, Jesus Christ the righteous: and he is the propitiation for our sins: and not for ours only, but also for *the sins of* the whole world" (1 John 2:1, 2).

This teaches then, that when one who has been justified by God because of the death of His Son commits a sin, he is accused before God by Satan. He is charged with having broken God's holy law and therefore worthy of death. Then Jesus Christ, the righteous One, steps in as attorney for the defense and pleads that His own death on the cross paid the penalty for the particular sin in question and therefore His client cannot be condemned. It is because of this advocacy by Jesus Christ that there can be no condemnation for him who is justified.

This advocacy is not in any way conditioned upon confession, repentance, prayer or anything else to be done by the one who sins. It says, "If any man sin, we have an advocate with the Father." It is well that it is so, for often unknown sins against God are committed of which the believer could not be cleared if he first had to do something.

This advocacy by Christ cannot of course enter into the life of any believer as an experience. It is something that takes place in heaven the instant that any child of God sins, and that is oftener than most people think. It would not be known except that it is revealed by the Word of God. The knowledge thereof, however, is of the utmost comfort and assurance to all who have come to see this great truth and realize how often even a saved person sins.

This too, then, is part of being saved by His life. More might be said on this subject, but that which has here been presented is sufficient to show the importance of this part of God's work of salvation. Because of it, one who has been saved shall be saved to the uttermost, or to the end, as Hebrews 7:25 might be translated. He shall be safe as long as his intercessor lives and that is throughout all eternity.

12

Objects of God's Unfailing Love

I T WAS shown (on page 53) that when the demands of God's justice have been satisfied by the death of Christ and an individual has accepted Him as the propitiation for sin, then the grace of God becomes sovereign in the life of that individual. From that moment on God deals with that person exclusively on the basis of grace. And as grace is the expression of God's infinite love, he becomes the object of God's love.

After God has justified a person there is nothing that can separate him from God's love. Paul exclaims: "Who shall separate us from the love of Christ? *Shall* tribulation, or distress, or persecution, or famine, or nakedness, or peril, or sword? . . . For I am persuaded, that neither death, nor life, nor angels, nor principalities, nor powers, nor things present, nor things to come, Nor height, nor depth, nor any other creature, shall be able to separate us from the love of God, which is in Christ Jesus our Lord" (Rom. 8:35, 38, 39).

The saved person is unalterably the object of the love of God and God deals with him on that basis alone. Let no one think that God ever becomes angry with one who has been saved. There is no wrath of God at any time upon those who have accepted Jesus Christ as Saviour.

God's love for the world gave His Son. To those

who receive the Son, God's love supplies all that they
need to fulfill His purpose with them under every cir-
cumstance in life. "He that spared not His own Son,
but delivered him up for us all, how shall he not with
him also freely give us all things?" (Rom. 8:32). The
"all things" are those that pertain to the Son and to
His kingdom and therefore do not necessarily include
material and temporal things. In fact, God might, and
often does, withhold from His children material blessings, that His spiritual blessings may become greater.

Suffering on the part of those who are saved can
be understood only as one sees that it is always confined to the realm of the material and the temporal.
In suffering, material or temporal things are with-
held or taken away. The body may become afflicted,
plans may go wrong, friends lost, and many other
things may happen. All of these are a withdrawal of
those things that come to man from God as from the
Creator to the creature. They are a part of His providence. When God's child so suffers, except through
his own violation of natural laws and otherwise because of his own neglect, then God withholds the
lesser temporal blessings of His providence that He
may better give of His greater spiritual blessings
from His grace.

The man born blind was so born that the works of
God might be made manifest in him (John 9:1-3).
Mary and Martha, whom Jesus loved, went through
days of deep sorrow ". . . for the glory of God,
that the Son of God might be glorified thereby"
(John 11:4). And Paul, who knew suffering, said; "I

reckon that the sufferings of this present time *are* not worthy *to be compared* with the glory which shall be revealed in us" (Rom. 8:18).

There is one definite provision of God's love for all who are His that causes suffering. It is known as chastening. "My son, regard not lightly the chastening of the Lord, nor faint when thou art reproved of him; For whom the Lord loveth he chasteneth, and scourgeth every son whom he receiveth. It is for chastening that ye endure; God dealeth with you as with sons; for what son is there whom *his* father chasteneth not? But if ye are without chastening, whereof all have been made partakers, then are ye bastards, and not sons" (Heb. 12:5-8 A.S.V.). This teaches that everyone who becomes a child of God is chastened.

To understand the meaning of God's chastening one must carefully notice a fine difference of meaning in three words; punish, chastise and chasten. All three imply visitation of distress and affliction upon a person, but there is a great difference in the purpose for which these are inflicted. Punishment is imposed because of guilt, because the law has been broken, and in order to satisfy justice. Those who do not accept Jesus Christ as the propitiation for their sins shall be ". . . punished with everlasting destruction from the presence of the Lord" (2 Thess. 1:9). This shall be that the justice of God might be satisfied. God never punishes His children.

Chastisement implies specific guilt, as under law, but the object thereof is correction and reformation of the offender. It is not satisfaction of justice as in punishment.

Chastening implies imperfection in the one chastened but never guilt. The purpose is not to satisfy justice, but always and only to purify from errors and faults. Gold is chastened in order that all impurities may be removed from it.

Chastening, then, is an expression of the love of God the Father. By it He visits affliction upon those who have been freed from punishment under the law, that they may be purified from that which is not in harmony with His holiness.

The purpose of chastening is that it shall yield ". . . peaceable fruit unto them that have been exercised thereby, *even the fruit* of righteousness" (Heb. 12:11 A.S.V.).

Another provision of God for those who are saved is that He, on their behalf, exercises all of His omnipotence. One who has believed is not left to his own resources to carry on. Paul in writing to the saints in Ephesus (and all believers are saints) said that he did not cease to make mention of them in his prayers that they might ". . . know . . . what *is* the exceeding greatness of his power" toward those who believe. Then he describes the greatness of the power that God exercises on their behalf. It is even the same power by which Christ was raised from the dead and set at God's own right hand in the heavenly places far above all principalities, and power, and might, and dominion, and every name that is named, not only in this world, but also in that which is to come:

and put all things under His feet. (See Eph. 1:16-23.) In all the Bible there is no greater description of the omnipotence of God than this, and it is momentarily exercised by God on behalf of every believer, even the most weak and failing. That power guarantees the accomplishment of His purpose in salvation.

Because God's love freely gives all things with Christ, and purifies from that which is out of harmony with Himself, and because His infinite power is constantly in operation on their behalf, there is in salvation a perfect provision for all who are saved.

13

The Eternal State of the Saved

MANY who call themselves Christians say that they are not concerned about the future state. What they are interested in is the present. The Bible, however, teaches that it is the future state that is of the greatest importance. In the first place the present life is limited to a span of a few years while the future is an eternity. Secondly, while there are glories of salvation to be enjoyed by the believer, even while in the present body, there is still the presence of sin and its consequences of poverty, sickness, death, and sorrow which will never be gotten away from during the present life. In fact the earthly existence of the saved man is but a period of preparation for an eternal state. Few there seem to be who realize the glories that await those who are saved and how exalted a position is to be held by them throughout an unending eternity. Finite mind cannot grasp the fullness of all this but the Bible reveals enough to show that it shall be the greatest thing that has ever come to any of God's creatures.

The eternal state for believers of this age shall be ushered in by the return of the Lord Jesus Christ. "For the Lord himself shall descend from heaven with a shout, with the voice of the archangel and with the trump of God: and the dead in Christ [all who are saved] shall rise first: Then we which are alive *and* remain shall be caught up together with them in the clouds, to meet the Lord in the air: and so shall we ever be with the Lord" (1 Thess. 4:16, 17). "We shall not all sleep [die] but we shall all be changed, In a moment, in the twinkling of an eye, at the last trump: for the trumpet shall sound, and the dead shall be raised incorruptible, and we shall be changed. For this corruptible must put on incorruption, and this mortal *must* put on immortality. So when this corruptible shall have put on incorruption and this mortal shall have put on immortality, then shall be brought to pass the saying that is written, Death is swallowed up in victory" (1 Cor. 15:51-54). This is the blessed hope for which believers are now waiting. When this shall have taken place then God by His work of salvation shall have removed every particle of the results of Adam's sin including corruption and mortality.

But there shall be much more than that. The saved shall forever "be with the Lord." This was His promise to His disciples; "I go to prepare a place for you . . . I will come again and receive you unto myself; that where I am, *there* ye may be also" (John 14:2, 3). Even before the foundation of the world believers of this age were of God the Father chosen in Christ to be holy and without blame "before Him in love" (Eph. 1:4). Jesus speaking to His Father said: "Father, I will that they also, whom thou hast given me, be with me where I am; that they may behold my glory, which thou hast given me: for thou lovedst me before the foundation of the world." (John 17:24). In the presence of God the Father enjoying His love in company with the Son of God and beholding His glory is the certain prospect of every saved person. But it is still more than that.

They shall not only be *with* Jesus Christ, they shall be *like* Him. "Beloved, now are we the sons of God, and it doth not yet appear what we shall be: but we know that, when he shall appear, we shall be like him; for we shall see him as he is" (1 John 3:2). ". . . as we have borne the image of the earthy [Adam], we shall also bear the image of the heavenly" (1 Cor. 15:49). For the Lord Jesus Christ ". . . shall change our vile body, that it may be fashioned like unto his glorious body" (Phil. 3:21).

To be conformed to the image of the Son of God suggests a position of great glory. And so it is, for the call by the gospel is ". . . to the obtaining of the glory of our Lord Jesus Christ" (2 Thess. 2:14). Though it has not yet been experienced by them, it has already been given by Jesus to those whom the Father has given Him. (John 17:22). And, "When Christ, *who is* our life, shall appear, then shall ye also appear with him in glory" (Col. 3:4).

But there is even more in store for those who are saved than to be free from the consequences of sin, to be forever with Christ, to be conformed to His image and to receive His glory. They are to enter into a perfect union with God. This is infinitely more than harmony. The angels are in perfect harmony with God, but they belong on a different plane. They are of another class. Jesus prayed to His Father; "Neither pray I for these [the disciples] alone, but for them also which shall believe on me through their word; That they all may be one; as thou, Father, *art* in me, and I in thee, that they also may be one in us" (John 17:20, 21). This can be nothing less than being elevated to the level of God, for only so can there be the same unity as now exists between God the Father and God the Son.

There are other declarations concerning the saved of this age which support this statement. "For we are members of his [Christ's] body, of his flesh, and of his bones. For this cause shall a man leave his father and mother, and shall be joined unto his wife, and they two shall be one flesh. This is a great mystery: but I speak concerning Christ and the church" (Eph. 5:30-32). Here the relationship between Christ and the saved is the same as between husband and wife. As a man and his wife must be on the same level so must Christ and the church be also. The ultimate for the saved then, is to be raised to a divine level.

If God had only saved man from sin and restored him to Adam's original state that alone would have been marvelous. To have done a little more and given him the position of an angel would have been greater. To have given to him the order of the archangel, or a seraph or cherub would have been still greater; but God does infinitely more than that, He raises the saved of this age even to His Own level.

Because the fact is so seldom recognized it is well to repeat that the marvel of this becomes all the greater when one remembers that Lucifer desired to be like the Most High and tried to bring it about by his own efforts. It was also the promise by Satan to be like God that caused man to sin and rebel against God. That which both Lucifer and man sought by self-effort and in rebellion against Him, God freely gives to those of His rebel creatures, who will but accept His Own Son as the propitiation for their sins.

So GREAT SALVATION!

14

Salvation Is of God Through Jesus Christ

BECAUSE of man's inborn sinful nature causing him to depend upon himself, he insists upon contributing something to his own salvation. It is the hardest thing for man to learn that he cannot do so. That is undoubtedly why the Bible at every point, reiterates the fact that that which is done in salvation is of God—God the Father, God the Son and God the Holy Spirit. It, therefore, seems needful to point out still further God's own emphasis upon the fact that salvation is of Him and Him alone.

To think that man can be brought back into fellowship with God and into union with Him by anything that man can do or that man can contribute is to fail to realize the awful gulf of separation between man and God that was caused by sin. Nothing less than God's work can span that chasm.

To hold that man can contribute anything toward being saved is to fail to understand that the finite cannot contribute to the infinite. It is to fail to realize the utter helpless and sinful condition of fallen man.

It is therefore necessary for all to realize with David, the Psalmist, that "Salvation *belongeth* unto the Lord" (Ps. 3:8); that "The Lord is . . . my salvation" (Ps. 27:1), and that, "He only *is* . . . my salvation" Ps. 62:2).

Salvation Has Its Source in the Love of God

God does not only love man. He is love (1 John 4:8). It is by such a One that salvation is wrought. That salvation is the expression of God's love is repeated over and over again in the Bible.

"For God so loved the world [i.e. mankind], that he gave his only begotten Son, that whosoever believeth in him should not perish, but have everlasting life" (John 3:16). As the measure of God's love is here said to be His Son, and He is infinite, so God's love for mankind is infinite and cannot be limited by man's sin. "But where sin abounded, grace [God's love in action] did much more abound" (Rom. 5:20).

The following passages declare that salvation is because of God's love. "But God commendeth his love toward us, in that, while we were yet sinners, Christ died for us" (Rom. 5:8). "In this was manifested the love of God toward us, because that God sent his only begotten Son into the world, that we might live through him. Herein is love, not that we loved God, but that he loved us, and sent his Son *to be* the propitiation for our sins" (1 John 4:9, 10). "But God, who is rich in mercy, for his great love wherewith he loved us, . . . hath quickened us [made alive] together with Christ" (Eph. 2:4, 5).

It is an expression of God's love that those who are saved are called the children of God (1 John 3:1) and His correction, or chastening, of His children, as was seen in Chapter XII, is also because of His love for them (Heb. 12:6). It is God's purpose that they shall throughout eternity be before Him in love (Eph. 1:4). And Paul declares in the most emphatic terms that nothing can separate those who have been justified, from the love of God which is in Christ Jesus.

Salvation, then, is a work of God for fallen man and is prompted by His infinite love. Is it not an insult then to God's love to hold that man must or even can do something, however little, to contribute to its perfection?

That salvation is of God alone apart from any contribution by man is evident from the source and the execution of God's plan of salvation.

Salvation was planned and purposed before the earth was created and that was long before God brought man into being. Believers were chosen in Christ before the foundation of the earth (Eph. 1:4). Eternal life was "promised before the world began" (Tit. 1:2). The death of Christ on the cross as "The Lamb of God which taketh away the sin of the world" (John 1:29) was "foreordained before the foundation of the world" (1 Pet. 1:20). Salvation was decided upon in the councils of God long before man came into existence. Surely man had nothing to do with those plans.

Regeneration, or being born again, by which man receives eternal life and enters the kingdom of God, (John. 3:3, 5) is of God. It is expressly said to be, "not of blood, nor of the will of the flesh, nor of the will of man" (John 1:13). As no man ever contributed to his physical birth so can no man contribute to his spiritual birth. When he is so born he is saved for all eternity because he has eternal life.

The Holy Spirit reproves the unsaved world of sin (John 16:8, 9). Christ has redeemed by His own blood unto God (Rev. 5:9). "God was in Christ [on the cross], reconciling the world unto Himself" (2 Cor. 5:19). It is God that justifieth (Rom. 8:33). The just shall live by faith (Rom. 1:17) but Jesus is the author and finisher of that faith (Heb. 12:2) and it is God Who works in believers "both to will and to do of his good pleasure" (Phil. 2:13). Believers are kept safe by the power of God and that through His own name (1 Pet. 1:5 and John 17:11). And finally, the Lord Jesus Christ shall change the bodies of all believers so that they may be fashioned like unto His glorious body (Phil. 3:21). Many more passages might be quoted, but these are sufficient to show God's own emphasis upon the fact that it is He Who saves man. Where in all this is there room for man to contribute anything? By the very nature of the things that are done that is impossible.

"The Lord is . . . my salvation."

"He only *is* . . . my salvation."

Through Jesus Christ

These are days of apostasy when the doctrine of the Trinity is widely rejected and the Unitarian idea, which denies the deity of Jesus Christ and teaches that salvation is by character, is being taught. It is therefore highly important to notice what the Bible teaches as to the place of Jesus Christ in salvation. It is impossible to consider God's salvation as offered in His Word without realizing that Jesus Christ is the Saviour and that salvation is through Him. But because of the denial of Christ's work in salvation it is needful to point out that apart from Him there can be no salvation for man. To reject that teaching is to reject the very central message of the Bible.

Jesus said to His disciples, "ye believe in God, believe also in me" (John 14:1). It is not enough to believe in God—to acknowledge that there is a God who created and provides for man. It is equally necessary to believe in His Son Jesus Christ. This is so because no one can come to the Father except by Him. He said, "I am the way, the truth, and the life: no man cometh unto the Father, but by me" (John 14:6).

He is the way; that is, the way to God. No man can find God apart from Jesus Christ. No man has seen God, but the Son of God. When He lived on earth as a man among men He declared God to man. He is the truth, and He is the life. To reject Him is to reject both truth and life and the only way to God. "He that hath the Son hath life; *and* he that hath not the Son of God hath not life" (1 John 5:12).

It has been told by a missionary to Congo that the natives of that land believe that there is a heaven and a hell. They also believe that it is impossible for man, because of his wicked condition, to go to heaven; he must to to hell. Therefore they worship Satan the ruler of hell. They offer sacrifices to him so as to lessen their punishment in hell. To them there is no way to God because they know not of Jesus Christ, the only way to heaven and the Father. They do not commit the error of those who hold the unitarian viewpoint, disregarding the only Way and seeking to go to God by their own merit. In seeing their own inability to please God, the Congo natives see the truth better than many who call themselves Christians.

Man, because of sin, has been separated and shut out from God. He can only come to Him by Jesus Christ. "Neither is there salvation in any other: for there is none other name under heaven given among men, whereby we must be saved" (Acts 4:12). "The Father sent the Son *to be* the Saviour of the world" (1 John 4:14). ". . . as many as received him, [the Son] to them gave he [God] power to become the sons of God" (John 1:12). "He that believeth on the Son hath everlasting life: and he that believeth not the Son shall not see life; but the wrath of God abideth on him" (John 3:36).

That there is no salvation apart from Jesus Christ, He who was truly Son of man and also Son of God, is further proved by the fact that the Bible, in speaking of the things that pertain to salvation, consistently makes mention of the fact that these are either in Christ, by Him, with Him or through Him. He is always related to that which God does in saving man.

The following are but a few of the many references to Jesus Christ in His identification with salvation. They show the vital part that He has in salvation. God's eternal purpose with regard to salvation for this age was purposed in Christ Jesus (Eph. 3:11). Believers were chosen in Jesus Christ before the foundation of the world (Eph. 1:4). God saves "according to his own purpose and grace, which was given in Christ Jesus before the world began" (2 Tim. 1:9). He is the "Lamb of God, which taketh away the sin of the world" (John 1:29). The exceeding riches of the grace of God in His kindness toward the saved is through Jesus Christ (Eph. 2:7). In the Son "we have redemption through his blood, *even* the forgiveness of sins" (Col. 1:14), and this is because He is the propitiation for the sins of the whole world (1 John 2:2). God has made peace through the blood of His cross, to reconcile all things unto Himself by Him (Col. 1:20). Believers are made accepted in the Beloved Son (Eph. 1:6 and Matt. 3:17), and are complete in Him (Col. 2:10). They are the workmanship of God "created in Christ Jesus unto good works" (Eph. 2:10).

There is not one conceivable thing that God does for man in salvation that is done apart from the Son of God, and God's Word is very particular always to mention that fact. There can, therefore, be no salvation to the one who has no place in his life for Jesus Christ as the Son of God.

If salvation is of God alone and His work is done exclusively through the medium of His Son, where is there room for any contribution on the part of man?

15

By Grace Through Faith, or, How Is Man Saved?

THERE is a very important question that comes to every person. It is this. How is it possible for any individual to enter into all of the things that are included in salvation? What must be done, if anything, to be saved? The Bible, when properly interpreted, gives a simple and definite answer.

Salvation is by grace on the part of God and received through faith on the part of man. "For by grace are ye saved through faith; and that not of yourselves: It *is* the gift of God: Not of works, lest any man should boast" (Eph. 2:8, 9).

By Grace

Grace is one of the greatest words in the Bible. It speaks not of what man does for God but what God does for man. It may be said to be God's abounding provision through the operation of His infinite, or unlimited, love on behalf of one who will believe in Him. It is the kindness and love of God toward man, whereby all that the Christian is and all that he has is provided through Jesus Christ. "He that spared not his own Son, but delivered him up for us all, how shall he not with him also freely give us all things?" (Rom. 8:32).

God is love and grace is that love in action.

Grace is always unmerited. In fact man's demerit is that which makes grace possible. Had man not sinned then Jesus Christ could not by the grace of God have tasted death for every man (Heb. 2:9).

The operation of grace is not hindered by sin, nor is it limited thereby. "But where sin abounded, grace did much more abound" (Rom. 5:20). "God commendeth His love toward us, in that, while we were yet sinners, Christ died for us" (Rom. 5:8). Some one has said, "Grace works not by what it finds, but by what it brings."

All that is included in salvation is by grace. It is not only that which God does to remove man's sin and guilt and restore that which was lost by the failure and sin of man. It includes *all* that God does in conforming redeemed man into the likeness of His own Son and placing him in a state of eternal glory.

Salvation in its fullest sense, including the past, present and future work of God for the believer, is one continuous series of acts of grace. "The Word [the Son of God] was made flesh and dwelt among us, . . . full of grace and truth. And of His fulness [of grace] have all we [who believe] received, and grace for [upon] grace" (John 1:14, 16).

It was by the grace of God that Christ tasted death for all men (Heb. 2:9). Sins are forgiven according to the riches of God's grace (Eph. 1:7). Sinners are justified freely by His grace (Rom. 3:24) and grace reigns unto eternal life (Rom. 5:21). Paul said, ". . . by the grace of God I am what I am" (1 Cor. 15:10), and God said that His grace was sufficient for him (2 Cor. 12:9). By grace there is deliverance from the power of sin in the life of the believer (Rom. 6:14). It is by

grace that the believer maintains a proper conduct toward the world and with fellow saints (2 Cor. 1:12).
Gifts for the perfecting of the saints and the work of
the ministry, for the edifying of the body of Christ
are said to be grace given to the saints (Eph. 4:7, 12,
13). There is grace by which believers may serve God
acceptably with reverence and godly fear (Heb.
12:28). Liberal giving of material things out of deep
poverty and under great trial of affliction, but with
abundance of joy is said to be a grace bestowed on
the churches of Macedonia (2 Cor. 8:1-4). And God
is able to make all grace abound toward believers; so
that they will always have sufficiency in all things
and may abound in every good work (2 Cor. 9:8).
There is grace to help in time of need (Heb. 4:16).
The heart becomes established with grace (Heb.
13:9) and God has given an everlasting consolation
and good hope through grace (2 Thess. 2:16).

In addition to all this there is the promise of grace
that is to be brought to believers at the revelation of
Jesus Christ (1 Pet. 1:13). Surely all this is grace upon
grace by Him who was full of grace and truth. Salvation is all by grace.

Not of Yourselves

Man can contribute nothing to his own salvation
because it is "not of yourselves." It is well that it is
so for man is fallible and finite and all that he does of
himself is destined sooner or later to failure. Therefore if he did add anything to accomplish his own
salvation his salvation would be imperfect and in-

complete. But salvation is entirely of God and that which He does is perfect and shall not fail. ". . . *it is* . . . by grace; [and therefore of God] to the end the promise might be sure" (Rom. 4:16).

When one considers the infiniteness of salvation, how could it be possible for fallen, sinful and undone man to contribute anything that might in the least be recognized by God as being given as payment for that which He freely gives or as contributing to that which He does?

Neither is it a matter of surrendering the life or the heart to God or yielding the life to Him. That is a part of sanctification and not in any way a condition for receiving eternal life. If it were necessary, salvation would be by works. There is, however, a surrender that must be made in order to be saved. It is necessary to surrender or to yield any and all dependence upon one's own righteousness as a means toward being saved.

As the essence of sin is man's desire to depend upon self and be independent of God, every effort of man to do something himself instead of completely depending upon God becomes just one more sin committed by him and keeps him from God.

The hardest lesson for man to learn seems to be that he can do nothing whatsoever to aid God in His saving work.

Not of Works

Salvation is also said to be "not of works." This is emphasized repeatedly in God's Word. "Not by works of righteousness which we have done, but according to his mercy he saved us" (Tit. 3:5). And again "Who hath saved us, and called *us* with an holy calling, not according to our works, but according to His own purpose and grace" (2 Tim. 1:9).

These passages most definitely exclude, as a means to salvation, all that can be called human works, such as obedience to the Ten Commandments, fulfilling the golden rule, joining a church or religious organization and participating in religious and social work. All religious exercises such as prayers, fasting, penance and self-denials, baptism and any other strivings on the part of man to earn or merit salvation are ruled out. Not that many of these things do not have a value in the sight of God, but they contribute nothing whatsoever toward gaining salvation and man's entrance into a state of eternal bliss with God.

It is not even a matter of putting away sin. That is a matter for the saved, or justified, person to do.

Salvation cannot be of works for then it could not be by grace. "And if by grace, then *is it* no more of works: otherwise grace is no more grace. But if *it be* of works, then is it no more grace: otherwise work is no more work" (Rom. 11:6). "Now to him that worketh is the reward not reckoned of grace, but of debt" (Rom. 4:4).

Lest Any Man Should Boast

Salvation is not of works lest any man should boast. This is so that no flesh shall glory in the presence of God (1 Cor. 1:29). How this puts to naught all the stories about men coming up to the pearly gates and being questioned by St. Peter as to the good that they have done to gain admittance! That is one place where man shall not glory in his own achievements.

The Gift of God

Salvation is the *gift of God.* It must be a gift to be by grace. Here again merit on the part of man is excluded, for that which is given on condition of merit or goodness is not a gift but a reward. Salvation then is not in the slightest a reward that God gives for good conduct. This again teaches that people do not enter heaven because of the good that they have done.

Through Faith

Inasmuch as salvation is by grace and is a free gift from God and is in no way of man nor because of any good or meritorious thing that man can do, it is evident that man's part in salvation is merely to depend upon or trust God to perform, and to accept that which God freely gives. That is exactly what the words "through faith" mean.

Faith is counting God sufficient to meet every need and able to do even that which seems utterly impossible. Abraham is called the father of all them that believe (Rom. 4:11). Of him it is said, when God promised a son, though contrary to all natural conditions; "He staggered not at the promise of God through unbelief; but was strong in faith . . . being fully persuaded that, what he had promised, he was able also to perform" (Rom. 4:20, 21). Abraham did not make the mistake of putting circumstances between God and himself but rather depended upon God to overcome that which to him seemed utterly impossible. This is the meaning of faith. From this it is evident that faith is opposed to human reason, for the latter considers circumstances and man's own judgments instead of depending upon the workings of an omnipotent and infinite God and receiving His revelations as found in the Bible.

It is also evident that faith is not work. In fact it is ceasing to work, for one who counts upon God to do that which He has promised ceases to depend upon himself to do that selfsame thing. (See Heb. 4:9, 10.) It is an acknowledgment of one's own inability to work. This is always an element of faith.

There is no merit in faith. *"It is* of faith that *it might* be by grace"* (Rom. 4:16). If there were the slightest merit in faith, it could not be a channel through which grace could work. It would be a counter agent to grace which, as has been seen, by its very nature excludes merit on the part of man. Faith does not only exclude the thought of merit, it actually includes the idea of helplessness and hopelessness. In faith one depends upon another to do that which one is unable to do for oneself. A child in the family is ill and near death. The family physician is called. In so doing the parents confess their own inability to deal with the illness and express their confidence in the doctor. There is no merit in calling the doctor. Their faith in the doctor merely gives him the opportunity to work.

To believe in God is to commit oneself to Him. In John 2:24 it is said that Jesus did not *commit* Himself to the Jews because He knew all men. The Greek word here translated "commit" is translated "believeth" in John 3:16 where it is said that "whosoever believeth in Him shall not perish but have everlasting life." This might correctly read, Whosoever committeth himself unto Him shall not perish, but have everlasting life.

It might be well to emphasize the fact that saving faith is not in a dogma or religious system but is in a Person. It is in that Person fulfilling His promise. Jesus said, "He that heareth My word and believeth Him [God the Father] that sent me, hath eternal life, and cometh not into judgment but hath passed out of death into life" (John 5:24 A.S.V.). Faith is also in the Son of God. "For God so loved the world that He gave His only begotten Son, that whosoever believeth in Him should not perish but have everlasting life" (John 3:16). It is also on the *name* of the Son of God. "But as many as received Him, to them gave He power to become the sons of God, even to them that believe on His name" (John 1:12). "His name" stands for all that He is and all that He did to redeem man from the penalty of sin. To believe in Christ and on His name is to receive Him as the One sent from God, Who came to save sinners and to give eternal life.

Faith then is not to believe things about Jesus, that He was a historical person, that He was a great teacher or a good man nor even that He came to be the Saviour of the world. There must be a personal dependence upon Him to save—a committal of one-self to Him. He came into the world not to *help* men to save themselves. He came to *save* that which was lost—that which was beyond all human help.

Again, faith is not a mere mental assent to the above facts concerning Him and His work. It is a heart relationship to Him. "For with the heart man believeth unto righteousness" (Rom. 10:10). Any real dependence upon God must come from the heart.

Jesus gave a clear illustration of what faith in Him means. He said to Nicodemus; "As Moses lifted up the serpent in the wilderness, even so must the Son of man be lifted up: that whosoever believeth in Him should not perish, but have eternal life" (John 3:14, 15). The Israelite in the wilderness (See Num. 21:5-9) showed his faith by looking upon the serpent of brass that hung on the pole. In this one act of faith was expressed a confession of sin and utter helpless-ness and an acknowledgment that God's provision was his *only* hope. He did not understand the signifi-cance of the serpent, nor why it was made of brass. He did not analyze his faith to see if it was strong enough or of the right kind. He did not question the intensity of his look. He surely claimed no merit for looking. There were just two things in his mind: his own absolute hopelessness and the sufficiency of God's provision, the object of his faith. And this is all that there is to that faith through which the lost are saved. There is no power in faith that contributes to sal-vation. The saving power comes from God.

One more illustration of faith might be helpful.

A traveler was taking his first trip across the Atlantic. During the first night out he was awakened from his sleep and immediately realized that he was far out at sea and the only thing between himself and death by drowning was the ship. It was a helpless feeling. The noon before he had committed himself to that ship because he had confidence in it. In that dark hour of the night he reassured himself of the trustworthiness of it and went back to sleep. So a sinner may depend upon Jesus Christ and commit himself to Him as the means of being brought to God, and can rest in full assurance of His trustworthiness.

Because faith is dependence upon God, it is clear that God's condition upon man to be saved is a return to the state of perfect dependence upon God which Adam had before he sinned. But in one sense it is more than that. Adam's perfect dependence upon God was as the creature to his Creator and Sustainer. In salvation, in addition to this, it is full dependence upon God's provision in Jesus Christ to take away sin and the consequences thereof and to give all things with Him.

Repentance and Confession

There are two elements of saving faith which need to be specially mentioned. They are repentance and confession. There are some who seem to think that these are not necessary for salvation. Others emphasize their importance to such an extent that they become conditions in addition to faith. Both of these positions are wrong. It is impossible to believe on

Jesus Christ as one's personal Saviour without repent-
of sin and confessing that one is a sinner.

For a sinner to repent of sin is for him to change
his mind concerning sin and there can be no dependence upon God to save without this change of mind.
As long as one sees nothing wrong in sin but finds
pleasure therein and is perfectly satisfied to remain
independent of God and His Son Jesus Christ one
will have no desire to be saved. As a part of dependence upon God for salvation one will think of sin as
the terrible thing that it really is. It will be seen as
disobedience to God, as contrary to His holiness and
as enmity against Him and most of all as that which
separates from Him. A real right about face regard-
ing sin takes place. If there be no such experience
one may well question the reality of the faith in the
Saviour.

To insist upon a repentance that in any sense includes the idea of remorse or a demand for a change
of conduct either toward God or man, as the works of
repentance preached to the Jewish nation by John
the Baptist (Luke 3:7-14) or as in penance, is to add
an element of works or human merit to faith. This
necessarily makes faith void because it is impossible
to depend completely upon God as long as one tries
to contribute something, however little, oneself.

So also in the matter of confession. It is impossible
to accept, or believe on Jesus Christ as the Saviour
from the penalty of sin without confessing that one
is a sinner and utterly unable to do anything to
remedy the condition.

One who thinks himself righteous needs no savior, in fact self-righteousness is the greatest hindrance to being saved. The Pharisees of Paul's time could not become saved because they were self-righteous (Rom. 10:1-3). "Jesus came into the world to save sinners" (1 Tim. 1:15). It was for sinners that Christ died (Rom. 5:8). Only by accepting salvation as a sinner can a person be saved.

To confess oneself as a sinner is not the same as to confess one's sins. It is far more fundamental and self-abasing. It is possible to confess many sins and still claim a great deal of human merit. To confess to God that one is a sinner is to exclude all human merit. Furthermore it is impossible for anyone to confess all of one's sins. Many have been forgotten and others may not even have been recognized as such. To confess part of one's sins and not all would be of no avail because all sin must be forgiven in order to be saved.

There is a place for confession of individual acts of sin, but that is for the believer who has committed sin and who seeks forgiveness. (See 1 John 1:9).

Any emphasis upon repentance or confession that gives to these the nature of being meritorious is in addition to faith and must be excluded for then they become works, and works, as was shown, have no part in salvation.

It has already been said, but can stand repetition, that the great difference between Christianity and all the religions of the world is that God offers salvation as a free gift of His infinite love to all who will but receive it from Him by merely acknowledging their need thereof and accepting, or claiming it; whereas every religion apart from Christianity demands some work on the part of man to earn favor with God. There is much in the world that is called Christianity which demands merit on man's part. This is not Christianity, and in so far as human merit is demanded, it denies God's offer of salvation by grace through faith.

God's Word says that salvation is of grace (God's unmerited favor), that it is received through faith (dependence upon God), that it is not of oneself, that it is the gift of God and that it is not of works, in order to exclude boasting because of human merit. Therefore, man certainly can do nothing but humbly receive it from God. All effort on the part of man to earn salvation by that which is in the least meritorious is dishonoring to God.

16

The Certainty of Salvation

L ARGE numbers of Christians go through life
without any certainty as to whether or not they
are saved. Many even hold that one cannot be certain
about this matter. Many others, while never ques-
tioning the fact of their salvation, are not sure that
they shall be kept safe from final separation from
God and from His judgments because of sin.

The lack of certainty as to the future is the cause
of much, yes, very much, of the world's economic
distress. Assurance is of inestimable value in all
phases of human life. So also in the spiritual life of all
who are saved, it has a most important place. Fortu-
nately, God's Word has not left man in the dark in
this important matter.

How Can One Be Sure He Is Saved?

All doubts and uncertainties as to whether or not
one is saved can be traced to one of three causes. It
might be due to man's proneness to consider his own
feelings. While emotions have their right place in the
life of one who is saved, they have nothing to do with
the fact of salvation. Uncertainty might also be due
to a feeling that one is not good enough to be saved.
Salvation never depends upon the goodness of man.
It depends upon the goodness and love of God and
man's acceptance thereof. Finally, uncertainty may
come from man's reasoning about salvation. As soon

as man begins to reason, he is off the ground of faith. As faith is God's only condition placed upon man to be saved there must be uncertainty when, because of reason, doubts take the place of simple faith.

When any man who is known for his truthfulness promises that he will do something, his word is accepted and his fellow men act in full assurance that he shall do as he has said. God is known for His truthfulness. He cannot lie (Tit. 1:2). "God *is* not a man, that he should lie; neither the son of man, that he should repent: hath he said, and shall he not *do* it? or hath he spoken, and shall he not make it good?" (Num. 23:19). Therefore that which God says in His Word can be accepted without the least hesitation on the part of man. God's word must always be the basis for knowledge about salvation. In speaking of salvation God uses very definite and clear terms which need no interpretation, but sometimes a re-emphasis because man's preconceptions blur their clarity.

One of the most definite statements concerning man's present possession of salvation came from the lips of Jesus. He said; "Verily, verily, I say unto you, He that heareth my word, and believeth him that sent me, hath eternal life, and cometh not into judgment, but hath passed out of death into life" (John 5:24 A.S.V.). Notice that the statement begins with a double "verily" as though it was necessary to strongly emphasize that which follows because of man's slowness to rest in the assurance that it is true. Then, in the words "I say" Jesus declares Himself as the authority for that which is said. The statements that follow must necessarily be accepted as the direct word of God, and true. To question them is to question the truthfulness of the Son of God.

Concerning every one that believes, Jesus said that he has eternal life. He did not say that he might or even shall receive it at some future time after death. It is a present possession of all who believe. As this life is *eternal* it cannot die. It is not mortal as is the physical life. It is impossible now to have eternal life and not be saved for time and eternity. This one statement should suffice, but it is followed by another. The one who believes shall not come into judgment. The judgment for his sins fell upon Jesus on the cross and therefore no judgment awaits the believer. One who shall not come into judgment *must* be saved and saved now. There is even a third statement declaring the present saved condition of one who believes. He has passed from death into life. This means nothing less than having passed from the state of being lost (death) into the state of being saved (life). It is an accomplished fact.

In view of these three statements, attested to by the Son of God Himself, there can be absolutely no question whatsoever as to the present salvation of every one who believes. The only question that can possibly raise a doubt in any person's mind is, Have I believed? To believe has already, in Chapter XV, been explained as meaning to depend upon God and to count on Him to do that which He has promised. It is to depend upon Jesus Christ as the propitiation for one's own sins as explained in Chapter VII and in-

cludes a change of mind as to sin and a confession
that one is a sinner and needs to be saved. It is an
intensely personal matter between God and the believer. Certainly, no one needs question whether or
not he or she has believed.

Can One Be Certain of Being Kept Safe?

The above passage not only gives assurance as to a
present salvation. It also assures the one who believes
that there can be no future failure in his salvation.
One who has received eternal life cannot die spiritually and be lost. One who shall not come into judgment cannot be lost because it is in the judgment that
the lost are declared to be forever separated from
God. One who has passed from death unto life has
passed from the domain of Satan (see Chapter V) into
the kingdom of the Son of God and that kingdom is
a sealed state (Eph. 1:13). It is not subject to change.

In viewing the greatness of salvation it was seen
that it could not be measured by measures applying
to creation, but only by the infinite terms applying to
God. If one who has been saved can be lost this could
not be true because there would be a time limit to
salvation. If a person remained saved for but a few
years, salvation would be but a temporal work. But
God says that it is eternal (Heb. 5:9).

All the things that God does in saving man are of
such a nature that the possibility of failure at any
point is shut out. Redemption from the penalty of
the law was with the incorruptible blood of Jesus

Christ. This redemption price can never lose its value. It assures an eternal redemption (Heb 9:12). One who has been redeemed can never again become guilty under the law.

Justification is by God counting the infinite righteousness of Jesus to the one who believes. There can never be found any flaw in that righteousness. This was made possible because man's sins were reckoned to the account of Jesus and He paid the penalty therefore. As *all* the demands of God's justice were then satisfied there can never be any charge brought against the person that has been justified.

When the justice of God has been satisfied nothing whatsoever can limit the operation of His love. All who are redeemed, justified, and reconciled to God are unalterably subject to His grace which is the full expression of His infinite love. They are the objects of God's infinite power, even the same power that He exercised in raising Jesus from the dead and setting Him far above all things in the universe.

By regeneration man is born into the kingdom of God just as truly as by the natural birth he has been born into the human race. That spiritual life which is born of God (John 1:13) partakes of the divine nature and therefore cannot sin (I John 3:9). It was sin that separated man from God. Because the spiritual life cannot sin, it can never be separated from God.

He who is born again is in a new creation in which the fixed law is, "grace reigns through righteousness unto eternal life by Jesus Christ."

All who are reconciled to God by the death of His Son shall be saved by His present life in heaven where He ever lives to intercede on their behalf.

As salvation is exclusively of God, as it is by grace and therefore unmerited by man, and as fallible man can contribute nothing toward his own salvation, there is no point at which there can be failure.

Salvation of one who believes in Jesus Christ is as certain and as enduring as is God Himself.

There are many passages in the Bible that declare the certainty of salvation but only one needs to be quoted here. "My sheep hear my voice, and I know them, and they follow me: and I give unto them eternal life; and they shall never perish, and no one shall snatch them out of my hand. My Father, who hath given *them* unto me, is greater than all; and no one is able to snatch *them* out of the Father's hand" (John 10:27-29 A.S.V.).

In view of all this, need anyone question his own salvation and whether or not he has been saved for all eternity?

Note. An exhaustive study of the security of the believer is found in "Shall Never Perish," by the author.

17

Why Does God Save Man?

WHEN one considers the awfulness of man's sin against God and God's omnipotence which includes the power to create another being to take the place of man, if and when he were destroyed by God's judgments, there comes a question that demands an answer. It is this. Why does God save man?

That Man Shall Not Perish

The first answer to this question is found in John 3:16. "For God so loved the world that He gave His only begotten Son, that whosoever believeth in him should not perish, but have everlasting life." Here God's purpose is in consideration of man. God knows, as no one else the awfulness of an everlasting destruction from His presence and from the glory of His power (2 Thess. 1:9) which shall be the lot of those who are not saved. His love, and that at the cost of His Own Son, would spare the creature from this punishment even though through sin he had become an enemy. The importance to man of being saved from perishing is so great that no one this side of eternity shall ever realize it, even in a small degree.

Unto Good Works

Some lightly and mistakenly say that to them salvation is more than "a fire escape from hell." Its importance to them is for the present life. It is true that one of God's purposes in saving man relates to man's life on this earth, but the eternal values of salvation far outweigh any temporal advantages as the infinite is greater than the finite. Furthermore, God's purpose for the earthly life of the saved person is that eternal values may result therefrom. In connection with the statement that salvation is by grace and not of works it is also stated that it is so in order that there may be good works by those who are saved. "For we are his workmanship, created in Christ Jesus for good works, which God afore prepared that we should walk in them" (Eph. 2:10 A.S.V.). God does not save man because of man's good works, but that it may be possible for man to do good works. Neither does God save man and deliver him out of an evil world and the power of darkness, to continue a life of sin as before. While God's ultimate purposes in salvation are eternal, the new nature given to one who has been saved is necessarily reflected in his present earthly existence. Paul said, "How shall we, that are dead to sin, live any longer therein?" (Rom. 6:2) and in writing to Titus he said, "I will that thou affirm constantly, that they which have believed in God might be careful to maintain good works" (Tit. 3:8). It was to be a *constant* affirmation by Titus that good works were to be *maintained*. Certainly God's purpose for the life of every saved person is that he do good works. Even His grace abounds toward the saved that they "always having all sufficiency in all *things,* may abound to every good work" (2 Cor. 9:8).

It is important to recognize just what constitutes good works. First of all, there are only certain ones who can perform good works. They are those who are "created in Christ Jesus" thereto. Only those who are saved can do works that God will accept as good.

Again, not all of the works by those who are saved are "good works." The "good works" of the saved were "afore prepared that we should walk in them." That which has been prepared by God beforehand must be according to His will and purpose. Therefore many seemingly good works by saved people which are self-willed and planned do not come under God's "good works."

Evidently these works, in order to be good, must be to the glory of God and not for the glory of man. ". . . whatsoever ye do, do all to the glory of God" (1 Cor. 10:31). "And whatsoever ye do in word or deed, *do* all in the name of the Lord Jesus, giving thanks to God and the Father by Him" (Col. 3:17).

Much of the present day social welfare work which is often prompted by deeply sympathetic feelings and carried out with much sacrifice cannot be included in God's good works because God is entirely left out. It is not done by saved people. The works are not "afore prepared by God" and the objective is not the glory of God. It cannot be denied that these works have an unmistakable value, but that value is a temporal one and has no relation to God's work of salvation which involves eternal values.

If and when the social work is done as a means of bringing to the needy not only temporal help but also spiritual and eternal aid through salvation, then it becomes "good works" according to God's purpose in salvation.

The good works are good because they have a part in the carrying out of God's whole program of salvation, and are not in themselves the ultimate objective. They are, as it were, a link in the chain of things that shall finally culminate in the praise of the glory of God.

To the Glory of His Grace

If God had only had in mind the matter of salvation from everlasting separation from Himself and unto good works, His work of salvation could have stopped far short of what it does. It would only have been necessary to have restored man to Adam's original condition in the garden of Eden. He could there continue in everlasting bliss and fellowship with God and carry on good works. But, as has been seen, God does far more than restore man to Adam's original state. Consequently there must be another and even far greater reason for God to save man. And so there is.

That it was the love of God that caused Him to save man suggests the possibility that in salvation God found a way to express His love as in no other way. Jesus in His prayer to His Father said; ". . . the glory which thou gavest me I have given them;

that they may be one, even as we are one . . . that the world may know that thou hast . . . loved them, as thou has loved me" (John 17:22, 23). That part of God's work of salvation through which the glory of Christ is given to those who accept Him is here expressly said to be in demonstration of God's love for them.

Ephesians 2:7 teaches that salvation is in order "That in the ages to come he [God] might shew the exceeding riches of his grace in *his* kindness toward us through Christ Jesus." Ephesians 1:5, 6 declare that the saved have been predestinated "unto the adoption of children by Jesus Christ to himself . . . To the praise of the glory of his grace."

"The heavens declare the glory of God" (Ps. 19:1). That glory is the glory of His creative power. When God's work of salvation has been consummated and they who are saved during this age have been brought into a perfect unity with God then shall there be praise, not only to the glory of His creative power, but to the glory of His grace. This is the very highest pinnacle of God's glory, and to accomplish this is the greatest reason why God in this age saves man.

Lucifer, in sinning, refused to give unto God His due glory. So also Adam and the entire human race, because of sin, have not glorified God as God. In saving man, His lost and rebellious creature, God does so, not only to restore the lost glory due Him as creator, but to gain a far greater glory, the glory of the Redeemer and the Saviour.

If man could contribute the least bit to salvation, by just that much would the praise of the glory of the grace of God be reduced. He could not be praised for that which man contributed. The glory of His grace must be absolute. It cannot be marred. An infinite God cannot be infinite if His glory is diminished by the slightest amount.

That is why human merit and the works of man are excluded as a contributing factor in salvation. That is why no flesh shall glory in His presence (1 Cor. 1:29) and that is why the basic principle of salvation is by grace through faith.

In salvation God does not salvage something that is good in man. He takes an utterly lost and condemned sinner, and raises him apart from any of his own merit to His own divine level and glory, all to the end that the glory of His grace may be praised.

Only as it is seen that the great purpose of God in salvation is to the praise of the glory of His grace, is it at all possible to understand why God does not destroy man (who in rebellion against Him tried to make himself like God) but instead actually transforms him into that exalted condition that he, in rebellion, sought to gain. There can be no greater manifestation of grace than that. Nothing could call forth praise to the glory of God's grace more than that action. Herein is also a reason why God permitted man to sin.

"O the depth of the riches both of the wisdom and knowledge of God! how unsearchable *are* his judgments, and his ways past finding out! For who hath known the mind of the Lord? or who hath been his counsellor? Or who hath first given to him, and it shall be recompensed unto him again? For of him, and through him, and to him, *are* all things: to whom be glory for ever. Amen" (Rom. 11:33-36).

18

Salvation and Man's Conduct

WHILE it is of the utmost importance to recognize that God says nothing whatsoever in His Word to the unsaved about the matter of conduct, and that salvation is offered as a free gift apart from the question of conduct, it is not to be assumed that there can be indifference in this matter on the part of those who are saved. God does not try to improve or reform an unsaved person because however much such a one might become improved, he still cannot measure up to God's demand for righteousness and thereby secure a standing before God as one who is righteous. Another reason why the unsaved are not urged by God to improve their conduct is that there is no power within them to live a life according to God's standard for those who are saved. The question of Christian conduct must, therefore, never be considered in relation to being saved. To do so is but to confuse the issue. After a person has accepted Jesus Christ as Saviour, and only then, does God appeal to that person in the matter of how his earthly life should be lived.

In salvation God freely gives to man a new position before Himself. Before a man is saved his standing before God is that of a sinner (a sinner by nature and because he commits sin) and he is under the condemnation of death. After he becomes saved, he stands before God entirely upon the merits of Jesus

Christ Himself. He is a child of God because he has been born again, and is every moment so considered by God. He is a member of the family of God. He is clothed in the very righteousness of God and nothing can be charged against him to alter that condition. He stands before God as the object of His unalterable love and full measure of His grace. This standing before God is entered into the moment a person believes on, or receives Jesus Christ as Saviour. Because it depends solely upon the merits of Christ, the position is the same for the most stumbling and failing Christian as for the most godly saint.

That it is possible for any man to so stand before God is known only because it is revealed in God's Word. It is never known because of one's experience. But because of his knowledge thereof the saved person enters into rich experiences.

It is the fact of this perfect standing before God that is always made the basis for God's appeals to the saved in matters of conduct. They are exhorted to live their earthly lives in harmony with their standing and with what they are in their saved state.

The following serves as a limited illustration of this condition. The children born into a royal family are taught and trained and exhorted to conduct themselves as royalty which they are by birth. They are an honor to the king only as they so conduct themselves. There are many things they cannot do that are not forbidden to other children. On the other hand, to the street waif of the lower east side of New York City there can be no appeal to live as a son of a king because he does not hold that position.

All of the writings in the Bible that are addressed to believers of this age hold with perfect fidelity to this principle. For every gift of grace there is an appeal to a life consistent with that gift.

It would be most inconsistent for those who have been delivered from the power of darkness and translated into the kingdom of the Son of God to continue to live according to the practices of their former state. So the appeal to them is, "For ye were sometimes darkness, but now *are ye* light in the Lord: walk as children of light . . . And have no fellowship with the unfruitful works of darkness, but rather reprove *them*" (Eph. 5:8, 11).

All who are saved have been redeemed from the penalty of the law by the payment of a ransom price, even by the blood of Jesus Christ. The appeal to godly living because of this reads, "For ye are bought with a price: therefore glorify God in your body, and in your spirit, which are God's" (1 Cor. 6:20). While it is contrary to human reason that God should give His Own Son in death to redeem man from the death penalty of the law, and can be explained only on the basis of love, it is most reasonable to expect that one who has been so redeemed and given an eternal position with God should spend the days of his earthly life so that God might thereby be glorified. This is not as a compulsion but because of what God in love has done.

Paul writing to the Christians at Rome, in a mes-

sage that also applies to all Christians of today, said,
"I beseech you therefore, brethren, by the mercies of
God, that ye present your bodies a living sacrifice,
holy, acceptable unto God, *which is* your reasonable
service. And be not conformed to this world: but be
ye transformed by the renewing of your mind, that
ye may prove what is that good, and acceptable, and
perfect, will of God" (Rom. 12:1, 2). Notice that this
which Paul urged the believers to do he called a
reasonable service." This was no small thing. Its rea-
sonableness is because of the "mercies of God." What
are these mercies of God? They are all that is related
to justification by the grace of God through the redemption that is in Christ Jesus because He was set
forth as a propitiation for sin (Rom. 3:24-26). Surely
one whose every sin has been forgiven and to whom
God has freely reckoned divine righteousness because
His own Son has died to satisfy His justice, ought to
present himself to God, renounce the things of this
world, and seek to live acording to the will of God.

In reconciliation, the saved person, who had been
afar off from God, is made nigh to Him. But many
who have been reconciled are not living in close contact with Him. It is not only their privilege to do so;
they are admonished to ". . . draw near with a true
heart in full assurance of faith . . . Let us hold fast
the profession of *our* faith without wavering; . . .
And let us consider one another to provoke unto love
and to good works" (Heb. 10:22-24).

He who is born again is born of the Spirit. The
Spirit of God dwells within him. Because of this con-

dition Paul could write to the Christians at Corinth; "What? know ye not that your body is the temple of the Holy Ghost *which is* in you, which ye have of God . . . ? . . . therefore glorify God in your body, and in your spirit, which are God's" (1 Cor. 6:19, 20).

He who is born again is a new creation in Christ Jesus (2 Cor. 5:17). Because of this he is admonished to ". . . put off concerning the former conversation [behavior] the old man, which is corrupt according to the deceitful lusts; . . . and . . . put on the new man, which after God is created in righteousness and true holiness (Eph. 4:22, 24).

Though some are not fully aware of it, all who are children of God have a blessed hope of seeing Jesus Christ their Lord and being changed into His image. This fact is made the basis for a strong appeal for a pure and godly life. "Beloved, now are we the sons of God, and it doth not yet appear what we shall be: but we know that, when he shall appear, we shall be like him; for we shall see him as he is. And every man that hath this hope in him purifieth himself even as he is pure" (1 John 3:2, 3). The unconditional promise to all believers to become like the Son of God should be the greatest possible incentive to godly living.

Unsaved men (and also many who are saved) think of conduct only in terms of compliance with a moral code. None of the above appeals is in the nature of such compliance. They are appeals to a new life on a divine plane, even while the saved are still on this earth. Only as a person realizes and enters into those things which come to him through salvation can these appeals have any meaning to him. That is another reason why conduct is not a matter for consideration until one has been saved.

In contrast to the above, under the law that was given by Moses, blessings from God were always conditioned upon that which man did. If he fulfilled the law God blessed him. If he failed to fulfill the law he became subject to severe curses. Both blessings and curses were faithfully predicted to Israel by Moses in his farewell address to them (Deut. Ch. 28).

There is much, indeed very much, confused thinking because the order under the Mosaic law is not distinguished from God's order under grace. Under law, because of the fact that the standing before God depended upon what man did, it was possible to lose one's standing and the blessings that went with it, and in the place of being blessed one became cursed. Under that condition the motive to conduct became one of fear of punishment. That motive to a very large extent underlies human conduct. It is the controlling motive in most lives. It is only natural that the unsaved man should think that fear is the motive for godly conduct, but when one who has been saved still thinks of fear of judgment as the impelling motive for conduct there is a great loss in that life. The motive to true Christian conduct is love. Paul wrote, "The love of Christ constraineth us" (2 Cor. 5:14). It is the love of God that gave His Son that whosoever believes shall not perish (John 3:16). It is the love of Christ who gave Himself to save the lost. It is the love of God by which all who are saved are called the children of God (1 John 3:1). It is divine love as expressed in all that has been done to save man and that is being done and shall be done to consummate the work of salvation.

That fear is not the motive for Christian conduct is clearly stated. "For ye have not received the spirit of bondage again to fear; but ye have received the Spirit of adoption, whereby we cry, Abba, Father" (Rom. 8:15). "For God hath not given us the spirit of fear; but of power, and of love, and of a sound mind" (2 Tim. 1:7).

Christian conduct, then, is the result of that which God does in saving man. Love, not fear, is the true motive thereto. These two are contrary, the one to the other. "There is no fear in love; but perfect love casteth out fear: because fear hath torment. He that feareth is not made perfect in love" (1 John 4:18).

19

What Does It Mean to Be Lost?

JESUS said of Himself, "For the Son of man is come to seek and to save that which is lost" (Luke 19:10). Paul writes, "But if our gospel be hid, it is hid to them that are lost" (2 Cor. 4:3). The word lost here applies to persons, and it tells of the state of these individuals in their relationship to God. Because Jesus came to seek them, it is evident they who are lost must be away from God. They have not received the benefits of the gospel of grace for the good news of a free salvation is hidden to them because their minds have been blinded by Satan, the god of this world (2 Cor. 4:4). As these statements are applicable to those who are not saved, it follows that all who are not saved are lost.

Men do not become lost because of anything they do. They are lost until they become saved. Only Adam and Eve became lost and in them the whole human race. Jesus Christ came into the world that men might be saved from their lost condition.

Inasmuch as those who are lost are not saved, to be lost means first of all to be without any and all of the great benefits, previously explained, that come to man through salvation. But it means more than that. Just as few realize how much is included in salvation so also only a few realize what it means to be lost and how terrible the destiny of the lost shall be.

God's Estimate of the Present State of the Lost

Salvation includes deliverance from the power of darkness (See Chapter V). Therefore, to be lost means to be in the realm over which Satan has sway and consequently to be outside of the kingdom of God. It is to be in that realm which as a whole is at enmity toward God.

God, in His Word, gives an estimate of the present condition of the lost. They are said to be dead in trespasses and sins (Eph. 2:1, 5). Death in the Bible always means separation. Physical death means the separation of the spirit from the body. Spiritual death means the separation of the spirit from God and the second death (See Rev. 20:14) means the everlasting separation of spirit and body from God. To be dead in trespasses and sins is to be spiritually dead—spiritually separated from God.

Someone has defined death as being out of correspondence with environment. To be spiritually dead is to be out of correspondence with God.

When Adam and Eve took of the forbidden fruit (Gen. 3:6) they died spiritually. Their sin separated them from God. Sin has ever since separated man from God. That is why those who are not saved are dead in trespasses and sins.

It is not only sin in the form of gross immoralities such as murder, drunkenness, adultery, falsification, bribery and the like, but many other things that are not even considered as sins. All that does not measure up to the perfection and holiness of God is sin. It is said; "All have sinned, and come short of the glory of God" (Rom. 3:23). Even the most moral and refined are separated from God by sin.

What is more, every man is a sinner by nature, because he is a member of a sinful race descended from Adam, the original sinner. Until any man has the sin question settled with God, he is separated thereby from Him.

What it means to be dead in trespasses and sins is learned from the changed attitude of Adam toward God after he had sinned. He hid himself from the presence of God among the trees of the garden because he was afraid (Gen. 3:8-10). Those who are spiritually dead are afraid of God. Something deep down in the heart, though at times dormant, causes the unsaved, as Adam did, to fear to meet God. Little do they realize that, as God in love sought Adam, so God even now in love is seeking them to bring them into complete harmony and union with Himself.

The lost are said to be without Christ, having no hope, and without God in the world (Eph. 2:12). To be without Christ is to be without the only means of coming to God and receiving His benefits. Jesus said; "I am the way, the truth, and the life: no man cometh unto the Father, but by me" (John 14:6). To be without Him is to have no hope as to the future state. To be without God is to be without the Creator and Sustainer of man and the universe. It is to be without God as Father. It is to be "far off" from Him (Eph. 2:13). Yes, those who are without God still en-

joy much of God's providence but they have no
claim upon His care and provision. They have no
standing before Him because they belong to a rebel
domain. It is only in the name of Jesus Christ that
any man can claim anything from God. Jesus said;
"Verily, verily, I say unto you, Whatsoever ye shall
ask the Father in my name, he will give *it* you" (John
16:23). The lost cannot ask in the name of Him
whom they have not received.

Those who are saved have been called out of darkness into God's marvelous light (1 Pet. 2:9). The unsaved are still in darkness. They are said to be "darkened in their understanding, alienated from the
life of God, because of the ignorance that is in them,
because of the hardening of their heart" (Eph. 4:18
A.S.V.). Men may be very intellectual as far as the
things of this world go but in darkness as to spiritual
things. The god of this world has blinded the minds
of them that believe not lest the light of the glorious
gospel of Christ should shine unto them (2 Cor.
4:4).

The unsaved are called the sons, or children, of
disobedience (Eph. 2:2). This is so because they
"obey not the gospel [or good tidings] of our Lord
Jesus Christ" (2 Thess. 1:8). Being disobedient to
the gospel and rejecting the Son of God they are "by
nature children of wrath" (Eph. 2:3). "He that believeth not the Son shall not see life; but the wrath
of God abideth on him" (John 3:36).

The above is not a very pleasing picture of the unsaved in their present state, but it is God's own description of their condition and is therefore true.

The Final State of Being Lost

Those who do not heed the gospel of the Lord Jesus Christ but reject salvation "shall be punished with everlasting destruction from the presence of the Lord, and from the glory of his power" (2 Thess. 1:9). This is an everlasting condition. In the present life there is opportunity to become saved and brought back to God, but when the final separation from Him has taken place there shall be no such opportunity.

This separation is not only from the presence of the Lord, it is also from His power and therefore from all benefits that go out from Him.

Many think lightly of being separated from God. They have nothing to do with Him now and do not admit that they are getting anything from Him. They think that they can do very well without Him. Little do they realize how much they are depending upon and receiving from Him every moment of their lives. The air they breathe was made by Him. The rain that falls and the sun that shines are both sent by Him. They call this nature, and so it is, but God brought it all into being and sustains it all by His power. Apart from God's providence for man, every creature would die instantly.

When man becomes separated from the glory of the power of God he shall not benefit in the slightest from God's providence. The creature will be completely separated from every phase of His provision. That state is called blackness of darkness for ever" (Jude 13). There shall be no ray of light to pierce the absolute darkness; no drop of rain to quench an insatiable thirst; no morning star to point to the break of a new day after that everlasting night.

Lost man, in that state is also described as being cast into the lake of fire. It is said that all who are "not found written in the book of life" shall be cast therein (Rev. 20:15). Some say that this is only figurative. If so, that makes the condition more serious, for the reality is always more than the figure. It is also spoken of as ". . . hell fire: Where their worm dieth not, and the fire is not quenched" (Mark 9:47, 48). And still again as ". . . outer darkness: there shall be weeping and gnashing of teeth" (Matt. 8:12).

All who are not saved are already under condemnation. "He that believeth not hath been judged already, because he hath not believed on the name of the only begotten Son of God" (John 3:18 A.S.V.). They are now living under a suspended sentence, but the judgment shall surely be executed unless they turn to God and in dependence upon Him receive Jesus Christ as their Saviour.

The essence of sin was seen to be a desire to be independent of God. The final state of the lost shall be one in which there can be no dependence upon Him. Hell, then, is nothing more or less than the fulfillment of man's desire and the ultimate consequence of his own action.

20

How Shall We Escape If We Neglect?

IN THE foregoing chapters the greatness of salvation has been pointed out. It culminates in nothing less than an eternity, not only in the presence of
God, but in the very image and likeness of His Own
Son and in perfect unity with God the Son and with
God the Father. It has also been shown that this salvation is available to all. It has been completely accomplished on behalf of man by God through Jesus
Christ. It is offered as a free gift to everyone who will
so accept it. The only condition imposed upon man
is to acknowledge his own individual need thereof
and accept it. Finally, the awfulness of the judgment,
even everlasting separation from God and His provision for man both as Creator and as Saviour has been
described. There is but one point left to consider.
That is the terrible possibility of completely losing
the benefits of salvation and suffering the awful judgments of God.

"For if the word spoken by angels was steadfast,
and every transgression and disobedience received a
just recompense of reward; HOW SHALL WE ESCAPE,
IF WE NEGLECT SO GREAT SALVATION; which at the first
began to be spoken by the Lord, and was confirmed
unto us by them that heard *him*" (Heb. 2:2, 3).

The first thought here is that apart from salvation
there is no escape from the judgments of God. Man

must accept God's salvation or he must face God as his judge. Having neglected that, he shall have nothing to offer as a valid reason to escape punishment.

The second thought, already mentioned, is the terrible possibility of neglecting God's great salvation. The word used in the Bible passage is "neglect." It is not reject. More people are lost by neglecting than by rejecting salvation. Probably only relatively few really face the issue and then willfully reject. Most people procrastinate.

When Paul stood before Felix and "reasoned of righteousness, temperance, and judgment to come, Felix trembled, and answered, Go thy way for this time; when I have a convenient season, I will call for thee" (Acts 24:25). There is no record of a more convenient season for Felix.

One of the great inventors of the past generation is reported to have said that he would give the last five years of his life to the study of religion. Without having received notice as to when those five years would begin, he died and that, as far as is known, without having given thought to the all-important matter of salvation.

The world is rushing headlong toward eternity without giving a thought to Calvary and the Christ Who there died that they might live. They are going to an endless death—a separation of both body and spirit from God and His love with all its benefits, all because they neglect to accept His great salvation.

With such great issues at stake, why do so many men, women and children neglect to consider and accept

God's free salvation? Why do some even go so far as to willfully reject it?

It seems safe to say that whatever the individual reason may be, it comes under one of two groups. The first of these is that men love darkness (John 3:19). Darkness as God recognizes it, is not confined to the things that are done by the underworld. Jesus came into the world to shine as a light in darkness (John 1:5). Apart from Him man is in darkness. This does not, as has previously been said, mean intellectual darkness, for there is much intellectual light in the world. It means spiritual darkness. There are many things in the way of culture, refinement, adventure, human progress and accomplishment which according to God's estimate are works of darkness. These things are not wrong in themselves but men love these things to the extent that they will not set them aside and consider the one all important thing: namely, salvation. Men love the pleasures of this world so that they neglect to consider their eternal welfare. This world does have pleasures to offer: preferment, honor, popularity, accomplishment, amusements and sports to mention only a few. But when this world shall pass away all these pleasures will have disappeared. They will have passed away even long before that time for each individual, whose days on earth have been numbered. There is nothing left. And what is worse, God's great salvation has been neglected until it is too late to accept it.

The other reason why many neglect God's great salvation is the belief that man can be saved through his own efforts. Many try to earn their salvation by their own goodness. They are often willing to suffer great sacrifices and deny themselves all worldly pleasures to earn God's favor and His salvation. In this effort on their part, they neglect God's salvation. As long as man fails to see the utter uselessness of even the finest human effort as a means to salvation so long will he neglect or reject God's salvation.

As has previously been mentioned, the Pharisees were not saved; they rejected God's salvation, because they went about trying to establish their own righteousness. There has probably never been any group of religious people more zealous for the true God than they, but they depended upon their own goodness and had no need for a freely given salvation from God.

The desire to obtain salvation by one's own meritorious works has its roots in man's unwillingness to acknowledge his lost and utterly hopeless state. Man dislikes more than anything else to admit that because of sin he is undone. He is unwilling to confess, as Paul did, that in himself "dwelleth no good thing" (Rom. 7:18). Men do not want to declare a voluntary bankruptcy in the court of the eternal Judge and list their assets at absolutely nothing and liabilities so great that they far exceed the possibility of human payment. They are not willing to write down "no value" against all of their own good works and accomplishments. They do want to offer God something in the way of a settlement even if it be but a fraction of one percent.

Whatever the cause may be, whether preoccupation because of a love for the things of this world, or an effort to earn salvation, the result is the same. Salvation is neglected and God's judgment is certain to fall.

That which follows has already been said and emphasized but it is of such infinite importance that it is fitting to repeat it here in different words as the closing thought of this book.

Men are lost because, and only because, they do not accept Jesus Christ Who is the way to God the Father, and apart from Whom there can be no salvation.

Men are not lost because they are not good enough for heaven. They are not lost because they belong to Adam's sinful race. They are not lost because of the sins which they have committed, however heinous these may be. They are not lost because they are born sinners. The condemnation that rested upon man because of all of these conditions was taken away when the Son of God bore that condemnation on the cross that was raised on Calvary's hill. He there, as the Lamb of God, took away the sin of the world. In fact He came to earth for that very purpose. Now, because sin was judged on the cross, God offers eternal life to everyone who will receive His Son as the One Who met all the demands of His justice. Those who will not so receive Him shall be judged and punished with an everlasting separation from the presence of God and the glory of His power (2 Thess. 1:9). ". . . he that believeth not is condemned already, **because he hath not believed in** the name of the only begotten Son of God" (John 3:18). ". . . he that believeth not the Son shall not see life; but the wrath of God abideth on him" (John 3:36). "For there is none other name under heaven given among men, whereby we must be saved" (Acts 4:12).

One day nearly two thousand years ago Pilate said, "What shall I do then with Jesus?" That question every man must answer. Man cannot escape it. He must accept Him, or he will neglect and thereby reject Him. There is no middle ground.

Some say, How can a loving God send men to hell? The question is rather, How can God, who in love has given His own Son to save men from hell, do otherwise than cast them therein when they reject His provision to save them therefrom?

How shall you escape if you reject SO GREAT SALVATION?

To anyone who has not yet accepted Jesus Christ and God's salvation through Him, there still comes the Bible's last invitation to mankind. **"And let him that is athirst come. And whosoever will, let him take the water of life freely" (Rev. 22:17).**